ARIANA GRANDE

STUDIO PRESS

First published in the UK in 2019 by Studio Press Books,
an imprint of Bonnier Books UK
The Plaza, 535 King's Road, London, SW10 0SZ
www.studiopressbooks.co.uk
www.bonnierbooks.co.uk

© 2019 Studio Press

Written by Liz Gogerly

Cover illustration by Keith Robinson

A CIP catalogue record for this book is available from
the British Library.

Paperback: 978-1-78741-477-8

Printed and bound by Clays Ltd, Elcograf S.p.A

1 3 5 7 9 10 8 6 4 2

MIX
Paper from
responsible sources
FSC® C018072

ULTIMATE SUPERSTARS

ARIANA GRANDE

WHEN DREAMS COME TRUE

For Raphaela with love

CONTENTS

CHAPTER 1

ONE LOVE

The sun was shining when Ariana entered the stage at Old Trafford in Manchester on Sunday 4, June, 2017. Dressed in a simple white sweatshirt with 'One Love: Manchester' printed across the front, ripped blue jeans and killer-heeled boots, Ariana dazzled as always. But there was something else behind her wide smile and sparkling eyes. There was sadness, determination, but, above all, love. As soon as the crowd saw her, there was a surge of excitement – love really did fill the air!

Take That, Robbie Williams, Pharrell Williams and Miley Cyrus had already taken to the stage at the One Love concert. Robbie Williams was in tears as he sang 'Angels' – at times, the crowd had to sing the words for him, just to get through the song. Then Pharrell and Miley had raised the mood with 'Get Lucky' and 'Happy'. But it was Ariana the crowd were here to see, and when she opened with 'Be Alright', they were joyful. She was back: singing, dancing, smiling and swinging that ponytail, like only Ariana could.

Later, she teamed up with Victoria Monet, The Black Eyed Peas, Miley Cyrus, Coldplay and even a local school choir. Throughout the concert, Ariana's love and admiration for the people of Manchester shone brightly.

For 'One Last Time', the whole cast of One Love Manchester joined Ariana onstage. Ariana looked around at the famous artists gathered at her side – how had it come to this? She did her best to push the memories of the tragedy just a few weeks ago from her mind. If she thought about that devastating night too much, she knew she'd break down and cry – and never stop! She hugged Katy Perry and Miley Cyrus. Somehow that helped to keep the tears from falling.

And all too soon, it was the final song of the

evening. Ariana walked to the front of the stage. The sky had darkened to midnight blue, but the lights from the rig shone brightly on her face.

"Thank you so much. I love you," she told the cheering crowd for the zillionth time that night – and she meant it. And then she closed her eyes and pulled the microphone in close, as the opening notes to 'Somewhere Over the Rainbow' played. Ariana began to sing. As ever, her voice took effortless flight as she belted out the well-loved song.

Wow! If only the audience knew how much this song meant to Ariana. Back when she was a little girl, she used to sing it with her grandfather. 'Grande' was her favourite person in the world, but he'd died a few years ago. He'd always told her to sing 'Somewhere Over the Rainbow' at the end of a concert. It hadn't happened yet... but this last week, there was a voice inside Ariana that told her this was the perfect song to close the concert tonight. And now that she was actually here onstage in Manchester, singing it, she could sense the spirit of her grandfather, right there beside her. She felt a lump in her throat...

When Ariana opened her eyes, she could see the crowd swaying, and twinkling lights and flags waving gently in the night air. The audience were starstruck and many of them were in tears. *Boy, it's hard to sing when you're about to cry*, she thought to herself as she stumbled over a few words. *But this is what love looks like*, Ariana realised, as her own eyes began to fill up.

It had been Ariana's idea to stage this emotional event. The bomb attack at her concert, in this city less than two weeks before, had shaken the world. Getting up and singing was the only way she felt she could help the victims of this terrible tragedy. The money they raised would help the families who had lost so much. And, by getting up and performing again, Ariana wanted to prove that love does conquer hate. That night, Ariana delivered her heartfelt message of love, and people applauded her for her courage and dignity.

CHAPTER 2

LITTLE PRINCESS

Ariana had been surrounded by love since that hot summer Saturday she was born in St Jude's Hospital in Boca Raton, Florida, USA on 26 June, 1993.

"A little girl..." whispered Joan as she clutched her newborn baby close in the hospital bed.

"She's perfect," cooed Edward when Joan passed him his new daughter to hold.

"*Bellissima,*" said Grande and he peered in wonder at the gorgeous little face of his new granddaughter, wrapped in a white baby blanket.

"Ahh, she has your beautiful eyes," Nonna added when she looked at her daughter, Joan.

"So like your eyes too, Frankie," said Joan, and she beckoned her son to come and look at his new half-sister, who was lying peacefully in her father's arms.

"What an angel." Frankie's voice was choked with emotion. He was already ten, which was so much older than this little bundle, but he felt an instant connection with her.

"We are going to be such super special friends," he said. "We'll have so much fun together."

At that moment, the baby's face screwed up and she opened up her tiny mouth as wide as it would go.

"*Aaaaaaaaaaah!*"

Everyone looked at each other in amazement – I mean, how did something so small make such an almighty sound?

"*Aaaaaaaaaaah!*"

She was weeny, but, wow, she was noisy.

"She's certainly got some pipes on her," laughed Grande. "I'll give her that!"

The whole family burst out laughing. The Grande-Butera family always had fun. And the love they had for each other shone out.

"What do you think we should call our princess, then?" asked Edward when he and Frankie were visiting Joan and the new baby the next day.

"She is a little princess, isn't she?" Joan's face went all gooey. "I've been looking at her all night and thinking of all the Disney princess names – please can we choose one of those as a name for her?"

Joan looked at them with pleading brown eyes. Edward and Frankie looked at each other. It sure wasn't what they had in mind but, actually, she was their little princess...

"What about something like Aurora?" Edward piped up.

"Yuk, that's just too princessy." Frankie winced and shook his head.

"Ariel," suggested Joan, looking hopeful.

"I'm getting a pattern here. You two seem to like your princess names beginning with 'A'," said Frankie.

"Actually, I always kind of liked Oriana from that film, *Felix the Cat*." Edward looked sheepish at his own suggestion.

"Mmm." Joan was not convinced.

"I got it, I got it!" Frankie was on his feet now, excited and extra pleased with himself. "Go with Oriana but change the 'O' to an 'A' instead. Call her... Ariana."

Edward and Joan looked at each other.

"I *love* it!" they said at the same time.

"Yesss! Ariana Grande-Butera it is," said Frankie, with his signature smile and eyes twinkling with happiness.

Within a few days, baby Ariana Grande-Butera was taken back to the family's home in Boca Raton, a Florida city known for its beautiful coastline and miles of sandy beaches.

"Boca really is the best," whispered Frankie to his sleeping sister.

Palm trees fringed the beaches and graced the gardens. Lush green parks provided shade from the hot summer sun. Frankie felt sure that his sister would love the place as much as he did.

"It's the most fantastic place to grow up in the world!" Frankie kissed Ariana's soft head. "I wonder what you will be when you grow up, little princess..."

"I think she'll be an opera singer when she's bigger," joked Grande.

Edward and Joan had a beautiful home in Les Jardins, a wealthy part of Boca. There was plenty of space for Frankie to run around and a swimming pool with a bar area for hosting the best pool parties. The house itself was tiled throughout, which had an extraordinary effect on any sound. The Grande-Buteras were a loud bunch, but every noise they made was echoed around the place because of those luxury marble tiles. And that included the cries of young Ariana.

"*Bellissima*, you are an angel, but those cries could fill a football stadium – let alone an opera house," said Grande.

That Christmas, the family gathered around the pool. As usual, it was sunny and it was wonderful to be together as a family again. Little Ariana was nearly six months old now and smiling at everyone – though mostly for her grandpa.

"How lovely to relax," said Joan as she lay

down on a lounger by the pool. "Work, work, work – that's all I seem to do sometimes."

It was true, Joan did work very hard. She was the chief executive of a telephone and alarm-system company, which she'd founded herself. The hours were long, but it helped to give the family the best of everything.

"Ahh – happy holidays, everyone," added Edward as he settled down near his wife.

He also worked very hard, running his own design company. Edward was very proud of it, but enjoyed time with his family, lazing around the pool.

"Hey, everyone," Frankie shouted. "Let's put the radio on for some Christmas tunes."

"Yeah!" – everyone agreed.

Frankie fetched the boombox from the kitchen and set it up on the bar. Then he twiddled a knob until he found the local radio station. Suddenly, the whole pool area was filled with the most extraordinary voice.

"Who is this?" asked Nonna, who loved music. "This girl can sing..."

"It's Mariah Carey," answered Frankie. "This is called 'Hero'. Do you like it, Nonna?"

"I don't like it," said Nonna with a twinkle. "I *love* it!"

"It's number one in the charts," Frankie added.

"Well, I think that deserves a dance, don't you?" said Grande to Ariana, who was sitting on his lap. And with that, he got up and twirled his granddaughter around the poolside.

"Aaaaa!"

Everyone stopped and looked at the baby.

"Aaaaa!"

This time she wasn't crying, she was singing!

CHAPTER 3

DIVA FEVER AND GIRL POWER

Ariana's grandparents had Italian and Greek roots – that's where the Grandes got their dark eyes and hair from and, her grandfather would say, their good looks, too! Perhaps it's where their passion for music and *la dolce vita* – the good life – came from, as well. Grande and Nonna especially enjoyed old musicals. The Grande-Buteras were lucky enough to have their own movie room, with proper leather cinema seats. It was great fun when the whole family got together with popcorn and soda and watched old classic movies together. Films like *The Wizard of Oz*, *Singing in the Rain* and *My Fair Lady* were favourites.

Ariana was intrigued by Judy Garland, the young girl who played Dorothy in *The Wizard of Oz*.

Oh, she thought, *I'd love to have a pair of red sparkly shoes and a tin man for a friend*.

And she just adored Audrey Hepburn, the cheeky flower girl who became a proper lady and danced at balls in *My Fair Lady*. Ariana would love to wear a gown like that and sing those songs!

Frankie was a natural-born entertainer and would often sing the songs from all those musicals to his little sister. Her face would light up with glee and she'd try to join in.

"That girl is going to be on the stage one day," repeated Grande, for the millionth time, as a toddling Ariana jumbled up the words of 'Somewhere Over the Rainbow'.

"As long as she doesn't grow up to be a diva," answered Nonna, who had a way of keeping everyone's feet on the ground in their exuberant household.

Grande regularly proclaimed that her brother, Frankie, would be on the stage one day, too. In fact, anyone who knew Frankie would have agreed wholeheartedly. Frankie was always belting out a show tune or power ballad and lighting up the room with his sparkling energy. You always knew when Frankie was home – the boombox would be blasting out the latest hits and he'd be singing along.

Frankie's kitchen parties were legendary. Before Ariana could speak properly, she would dance around, humming and warbling along to Madonna, Mariah Carey, Celine Dion and the Spice Girls.

"Hey, let's put Whitney on again, Ari." Frankie picked his little sister up and the pair of them performed their own special duet to 'I Will Always Love You'. Whitney could hit the high notes and dive down to the low ones too, and her emotional delivery sent shivers down their spines. Frankie and Ariana's version was very loud and much funnier.

"You know, listening to Whitney makes me tingle," said Nonna. "But you two just make me giggle!"

Frankie and Ariana were always up to something. And, when she wasn't working, Joan was always happy to join in. Joan wasn't your average mother.

She mostly wore black clothes, even in the blazing Florida heat, and she had a fascination with horror films. While most mums let their kids watch *Sesame Street* or *Bear in the Big Blue House*, Joan was letting hers watch *The Addams Family* or old horror movies. It didn't take long for Ariana to get into the scary stuff, too.

"Why is it so dark and quiet in here?" Edward shouted one day as he shut the front door. He was late home from work and expected to find all the lights on, music blaring and the usual madness going on.

"Oooooooohhh!"

What was that spooky sound?

"Who's there?" Edward spoke into the darkness.

"Ooooooooooohhhhhh!"

There it was again! But it was definitely the voice of young child this time.

"Oh, what is going on now?" Edward was a bit annoyed.

"Boo!" Joan and Ariana appeared from behind the couch. They were both made-up to look like skeletons.

"Oh, you two," gasped Edward. "You drive me

crazy with this freaky stuff! It isn't even Halloween."

"Nope," said Joan. "It's just another Wednesday night at the Grande-Buteras!"

Joan and Ariana also enjoyed a good sing-song in the car. One sunny day, they were driving along when 'I Want You Back' by NSYNC came on the radio. Ariana was always singing, but today she was really hitting the notes.

"Is that you?" asked Joan when she realised it was Ariana who was sounding so extraordinary, not the band!

"Yeah, Mommy," answered Ariana, who had no idea she'd done anything special.

"Can you do that again?"

So Ariana did. Car journeys were never the same again...

All this singing, dancing and dressing up was heading somewhere, but who knew where? Aged four, Ariana already had ideas of her own.

"What is a diva, Frankie?" she asked her big brother. She'd heard Nonna use the word and she was curious.

"Hmm. I think it's a singer, but I'm not sure..."

Frankie decided they should look it up in the dictionary. He grabbed one from Mom's office and flicked through the pages until he arrived at the entry:

diva

noun

    1. a celebrated female opera singer.

    2. a famous female singer of popular music.

    3. a self-important person who is temperamental and difficult to please (typically used of a woman).

"Well, that's interesting," said Frankie. "Maybe one day, you *will* be a diva, little sis."

"What do you mean, Frankie?" She looked puzzled. "Will I be an opera singer, a pop singer or an important person?"

"You'll be a pop singer of course, Ari!"

Not long afterwards, Ariana picked up the phone, called 411 (the operator) and asked to be connected to the Nickelodeon satellite channel.

The famous children's television station showcased loads of kids who could sing and perform. Ariana was determined to be one of them and star on the live-action comedy show called *All That*.

"Well, honey," said the receptionist who answered her call, "are your mommy and daddy around?"

"No," answered Ariana.

"Well, dear, I think you need an agent."

Ariana was puzzled. Why would she need a spy to help her to become a pop star?

CHAPTER 4

BEACH DAYS, HOCKEY CRAZE

At the weekends, the family would pack up the car, whizz down Spanish River Boulevard and be on the silky sands of Boca Raton in less than ten minutes. In the summer, the turquoise sea was so beautiful and there were palm trees for shade. Sometimes, they would take a picnic and hide out in the sand dunes for the day. "Over here, Ari," Frankie would shout as he dived from the dunes and beckoned his fearless sister to join in.

Ari also loved playing in the waves and swimming through the warm water. Sometimes she would get spooked, though, and shiver with fright. What was that she saw in the water? Could it be...? Was it an actual real-life shark? Luckily, it was always just Ariana's imagination playing tricks on her.

Those long days at the beach were amazing, but there was always that silent dread there may be sharks lurking in the water. Ariana loved sea animals – tiny seahorses and their cute blinking eyes were her absolute favourite, but sharks both fascinated and freaked her out in equal measure.

"I can't believe you love this *Jaws* film so much." Edward really did wonder about his daughter sometimes. "Sharks petrify you, so why do you *keep* watching it?"

"It's the best film ever, Dad," Ariana explained. "I love feeling scared."

Ariana and her friends had great fun doing their own version of the scary scenes, at the beach at Boca Raton or in the pool round at Ariana's house.

"*Aaarrrghh! AAARGH!*"

There were those loud, piercing shrieks from the pool area again.

"Can you guys stop screaming?" shouted Edward. "I can't think straight."

"It's alright, Dad," Ariana called back. "We're

practising for my *Jaws* party. It's going to be so awesome."

"*Jaw*-some, more like," laughed Edward. "Why do you love all this blood and horror stuff so much, Ari?"

"At least it isn't a *Nightmare on Elm Street* party, Dad – I've got the mask and everything, but even Mom said no to that!"

Joan didn't say no to going to see *The Rocky Horror Picture Show* at the theatre, when Ariana was seven, though. Ari was probably the youngest person there, but for her it was one of the best nights ever. She got to put on freaky make-up and wear loads of black – just like her mum. Frankie and Joan looked hilarious in their torn stockings and gothic gear. But the highlight of the evening had been singing and giggling along to the 'Time Warp'.

Edward didn't do horror, but he loved hockey – ice hockey, that is. He was a massive fan of the local team, the Florida Panthers. Ariana was only five when she went to her first match. Her jaw dropped as she watched the players swish around the pitch quickly, hitting the puck at frightening speeds. It was so exhilarating and she became a regular at every home game.

During one match, Gord Murphy accidentally hit a puck into the crowd. It whistled through the air towards Ariana and her family.

"Owwwwww!"

"Oh, honey, are you OK?" asked Joan, looking anxiously across at her daughter. "Did it hit you?"

Ariana was holding her right wrist and her big brown eyes were watering.

"Yes," Ariana sobbed. "It got me on the wrist... but I'm fine."

After the match, the team apologised to their young fan and gave her one of their jerseys.

"Don't worry, Ari," her mum reassured her as they sat watching another match a few months later. "Pucks don't get hit into the crowd like that very often. You were very unlucky."

Just then, another puck flew off the court and hit Ariana on the left wrist.

"OWWWWW!"

Quickly, Edward and Joan whisked her off to the first-aiders, to make sure there were no broken bones.

"What are the odds of that happening?" Edward shook his head in disbelief.

"Luckily, it's just another bruise," said Joan, giving Ariana a kiss on her head.

It did hurt, but the club were quick to find a way to say sorry for the accident.

At the next match, Ariana was allowed to ride on the ice resurfacer as it circled the pitch turning water into ice and creating the perfect surface for skating.

"Just look at her," beamed Joan. "She looks like a princess..."

Ariana was beside herself with excitement, waving to all the crowd as the machine glided around the rink.

"Hmm," agreed Edward. "She certainly likes the limelight!"

When Ariana wasn't showing off with a crowd of friends, she was larking around at home in front of the camera. Having a father with a design company was useful because he was interested in photography and cameras – but, best of all, video cameras! From an early age, Ariana was delighted to dress up and perform in front of the camera. All that jumping around in the living room or in her bedroom was like a dress rehearsal for... who knew what?

Ariana began making music at home, too.

"Ariaaanaa," Joan's voice floated up the stairs. "You should be in bed now."

Ariana pretended she hadn't heard. She was in her favourite room of the whole house: the recording studio. It was next door to her bedroom, so she could easily creep in there at any time.

Ari was sitting at the keyboards, trying out different chords and composing her own tunes. She hadn't had any proper music lessons yet, but at school the teachers said she had a natural ear for music. Ariana closed her eyes, as she played the keyboards and began to sing. With her eyes softly shut, she could escape into the world inside her head where the only thing that mattered was the music she was making. It was a magical feeling – the best feeling – and she wasn't going to let her mother ruin it by telling her it was time for bed!

The Grande-Butera household had always been a happy, fun place to be. Friends and family were always welcome. So it came as a great surprise when Edward and Joan began to drift apart.

"Are Mom and Dad going to split up?" Ariana asked Frankie.

"I just don't know," admitted Frankie. "Dad works so hard, and he's never around..."

"Oh, Frankie." She looked so sad. "I just want us all to be happy – I can't bear the idea of our family not being together..."

CHAPTER 5

GIRLS KEEP SINGING

When the going gets tough, the tough get going – and when the going got tough at home, Ariana kept singing! Grandpa and Nonna loved to hear her belt out the classics.

"Give us a song."

Grande was so proud, he'd get Ariana to sing for friends and family all the time.

At school, Ariana was picked out for lead roles in the Christmas shows, and she was always the winner if there was an *X-Factor*-style event at school.

"You've got a special talent," her teacher kept telling her. "If you can focus on using your voice just for singing, you'll go a long way."

It was true, Ariana did do rather a lot of giggling in class, but she just couldn't help herself – laughter was in her blood, too!

As she turned eight, Ariana discovered that her urge to perform was growing and growing. The night she stepped onto the ice rink at the Florida Panthers v Blackhawks match at the club in Sunrise it just got bigger. This time, she was under the glare of a spotlight, with a microphone right under her nose and TV cameras perched before her.

Ariana had the worst case of butterflies of her life, but anyone watching on TV or from the crowd could only see a bright-eyed young girl who looked incredibly calm. She'd been chosen to sing the national anthem of the USA before the game. Ariana was shaking, but she was determined to do her best in front of the massive crowd and live cameras.

As she began singing, those flutters faded away and the words flowed effortlessly. Her nerves didn't get the better of her as her voice rang out, sweet and pure until near the end of the song, when she belted out the words.

Ariana held the final note, and the crowd cheered in admiration – for a little girl, she sure could sing!

Ari grinned so hard she thought her mouth would break.

"Nicely done, young Ariana Grande-Butera," announced the host.

Wow, thought Ariana. *This is what I'm born to do...*

"Ariana, it's time for bed."

Joan lost count of the times she told her daughter to go to bed rather than sit at the keyboards in the studio. But even when Ariana did climb into bed, she'd sing herself to sleep. Lying in the dark, she'd practise different ways of singing or try out new tunes in her head. Singing became as natural to Ariana as breathing. And even when she was asleep, Ariana dreamed about singing. Often she'd be onstage, singing in front of an adoring audience.

Ariana wasn't sure how she was going to make her dreams come true, but every day she practised in the studio or messed around with Frankie, who had now left school and was auditioning for parts in musicals.

"Do you believe in magic?" she asked Frankie one day when they were in the kitchen together.

"What, like in that *Harry Potter* book you love?" Frankie laughed.

"Yeah! I could do with a spell that will transform me from an ordinary schoolgirl into a superstar."

"Here you go..." Frankie reached for a wooden spoon from the kitchen drawer and waved it around. "*Vera verità*, or whatever they say..."

"Oh dear." Ariana pinched herself and giggled. "I'm still me..."

Not long after that, Ariana was back onstage. And the thrill was as strong as ever.

"Your turn now." Frankie gave Ariana the book of karaoke songs to look through. "There's loads of Mariah Carey and Madonna to choose from..."

The family were on a cruise together, and every night the Grande-Butera kids got up and took a turn at the karaoke. After dinner one night, Ariana did a song by one of her favourite stars, Celine Dion. 'My

Heart Will Go On' from the film *Titanic* was not a typical choice for a young girl, but Ariana gave it everything she had – and more!

Nobody there that evening had expected a little girl to have such a powerful voice. One spectator was so impressed that she came over to the Grande-Buteras' table to talk with Ariana.

"Hello. You have an incredible voice." The glamourous passenger beamed at her. However, this was no ordinary traveller – this woman was Gloria Estefan!

Frankie's jaw dropped in amazement. Gloria was mega famous and had sold over 100 million records of her own, including the famous 'Rhythm is Gonna Get You' – a song they'd all shimmied to in the kitchen at home!

"Why, thank you..." Ariana was taken aback.

"You're very talented!" Gloria exclaimed.

"What an enormous compliment, Ari." Joan was so proud of her girl.

"You must keep on singing – it is what you're supposed to do." Gloria looked Ariana straight in the eyes. "Don't ever give up!"

Ariana, give up? What an idea... Everyone, including Gloria Estefan, had told her she was a natural – that she was destined to be a singer. Inspired by her brother's interest in musical theatre, she joined a local youth theatre group in Boca, where she soon found a gang of like-minded friends who were mad about musicals, too.

Some weekends, they'd travel up to New York to see shows on Broadway. At other times they would come over to Ariana's and watch musicals in the movie room. It was great to hang out with kids who were as geeky about those old classics as she was! Her new friend Aaron Gross was into *Harry Potter*, too. They'd mess around, pretending to be Harry and Hermione, putting spells on everyone and everything!

"I'm going for it, Aaron!" Ariana confided in her friend one day. "I want to be Annie."

"Ahh, no more Hermione, then?" Aaron laughed. "That's the main part, but I think you could do it, Ari."

Ariana had been obsessing about the role ever since she heard that their theatre group would be putting on a production of the musical *Annie*. Ariana loved the film, and she watched it over and over in the movie room to get ideas about how to play the little orphan, Annie.

Life at home had been weird recently. Ariana's parents were still arguing. The only way to escape the stress of it all was to think about the role, or disappear to the studio and practise singing. Right now, if she could choose any *Annie* song for the audition, she knew she could pour her heart and soul into 'It's the Hard-Knock Life'. However, everyone expected you to sing 'Tomorrow' – it was Annie's famous solo in the film. If she could nail that song, Ariana knew she could blow them away at the audition...

CHAPTER 6

IN THE SPOTLIGHT

On the way to the audition, Ariana felt nervous – in fact, she was so wobbly and worried that she nearly threw up in the car! Nevertheless, she pulled herself together, and got up and sung 'Tomorrow' with a few shakes but no mistakes.

"That was beautiful!" exclaimed one of the directors as she clapped enthusiastically.

"I think we've found our Annie," whispered the other.

Nobody in the family had expected Ariana to get the lead role in her first production.

"I got it, I got it! They want me to be Annie!" She flung herself into her grandfather's arms.

"Aww, *bellissima*." He hugged her tight. "I'm proud of you!"

Joan was delighted but concerned. Ariana was still only eight years old and Joan didn't like leaving her young daughter alone at the rehearsals. In the end, the only way to make it happen was for Joan to take part in the play herself. Joan wasn't an actress, but she'd do anything for Ariana – even if that meant playing the part of Daddy Warbucks's maid.

And so it was that Ariana Grande-Butera was ready to make her stage debut at the Little Palm Family Theatre in Boca in 2001. The curly red wig she wore was hot under the stage lights, but it immediately transformed Ariana into the character of Annie, who many people knew and loved. The raggedy clothes and dirt on her face completed the look. But how would Ariana sound when she got up to perform in that small playhouse?

As she stepped onstage, Ariana didn't dare look at the crowd in case she fluffed her words. It was much easier to pretend there was no one there and she was all alone, an orphan looking for love and hope in a strange new city.

Her sweet voice suited 'Tomorrow' and, surprisingly for such a little girl, her voice filled the theatre. As she sang it, all eyes in the house were drawn to Ari – with her impish smile, she really was the cutest thing.

Ariana didn't have to look at the crowd to know they were enjoying her performance. There was a buzz of excitement in the air and she felt its force – like a huge wave crashing on the beach but deep inside herself.

The words of the song were so familiar and Ariana hit every single note. As 'Tomorrow' ended, there was an ecstatic round of applause.

Edward didn't miss a single performance.

"That was wonderful, Ari," he gushed.

"You're amazing, my darling!" Joan exclaimed.

Nonna captured the whole thing on video and showed it to all of her friends.

"I'm so proud of you, I can't help myself," she admitted. "I'm a real show-off when it comes to you!"

Frankie made a loud announcement to the crowd on the night he was there.

"My little sister is going to be a star!" He glowed with pride. "Remember, I said it first!"

"No, you didn't," Grandpa reminded him. "I did – the day she was born!"

Ariana loved every second of the whole experience – even signing autographs.

"The only sad bit is that it has to end," she told her mum. "It's gone far too quickly."

The family celebrated with a meal at Ari's favourite restaurant in Boca. Stir Crazy served the best chicken, tofu and brown rice in the land, as far as Ari was concerned. It felt good to have all of her family together – overexcited, noisy and laughing like crazy. It was such a shame that had to end, too...

"I wish I could put a spell on our family," Ariana confided to Aaron one day. They had become much closer since the production of *Annie* and she often confided in her 'showbiz' friend.

"Oh, I see, Hermione is back!" he said.

"It'll take more than *Harry Potter* magic to sort us out." Ariana's eyes filled up with tears.

"What do you mean?" asked Aaron gently. "You have the perfect family."

Ariana shook her head. "Mom and Dad are going to get divorced."

"Oh no, Ari." Aaron hesitated. "I'm so, so sorry."

"I know. I can hardly sleep or eat."

"What, not even chocolate ice cream with rainbow sprinkles?" Aaron knew that was her favourite.

"Nope." Ariana's nose had gone red now – those tears were going to fall at any moment. "I'm lucky, I guess..." Ariana searched for the positives. "I have Grande and Nonna. They love me always." It was true. They still came over all the time, and they would curl up and watch the old musicals with the children.

"Sounds good," Aaron smiled.

"Yeah," Ariana looked thoughtful. "It just seems that life will never be the same again."

Life did change. But to get through the sad times, Ariana threw herself into music and song. She signed up for every production going at the local theatre group. She didn't care whether she had the lead part or she was one of the chorus, as long as she was up on the stage.

At a time when things felt so tragic, Ariana discovered her own kind of magic.

CHAPTER 7

LIFE GOES ON

Life wasn't always singing and performing – Ariana had to go to school, like everyone else. Joan and Edward worked hard and decided to put their children through private education. From the age of ten, Ari attended Pine Crest School in Boca Raton, like Frankie had.

"You'll love it here," Frankie reassured Ari on her first day. "They do loads of singing and dancing. And just wait till you see the performing and visual arts department."

"I'm into science too, Frankie!" Ariana wailed. "Does it have a science lab?"

"Yes," laughed her brother. "And the library is stacked with *Harry Potter* and *Lord of the Rings* books, so you'll get all the magic and monsters you love, too."

"I can't wait." Ariana skipped towards the gates feeling really happy.

"And, at lunchtime," Frankie called, "everyone gets on their broomsticks and plays Quidditch! Ari, you'll have a *fabulous* day."

And she did – Ariana liked school, and although she was mischievous and enjoyed a giggle in class, she was a good student. Ariana's only disappointment was that she never got to play Quidditch!

You could always hear Ariana laughing when she was around her school friends Suzanne, Aaron, Michael and Christie. They'd think up pranks, film themselves singing and making jokes, or just hang out gaming or playing Monopoly. Suzanne and Ariana regularly ended up in each other's bedrooms making videos, and often found themselves in an uncontrollable fit of giggles.

And she didn't only have a laugh with her friends. Grande and Nonna encouraged her to do stand-up comedy and impersonations.

"Go on, Ari, do your Mariah Carey for us, honey," asked Nonna.

"Oh my, I'm not sure I can." Ariana was getting good at mimicking other singers, but it was hard work doing Mariah or Whitney.

"You can do 'em all," encouraged Grande. "And you're a whole lot better than any of them... "

"Oh, you." Ariana giggled. "OK, here goes..."

Grandpa's eyes beamed with pride as Ariana sang 'I Will Always Love You' – she wasn't a teenager yet, but she had an incredible range and enough emotion to carry the song.

Out of school, life was filled with all the usual activities – going to the beach, visits to the local climbing wall or just hanging out at the mall, shopping for new clothes in Ariana's favourite shades: peach and periwinkle. Ariana never forgot that she was fortunate to have such a loving family – even though her parents had now separated – as well as fabulous friends, a big home with a pool and everything a young girl could ever really want.

Joan always reminded her children they were lucky and that they should give something back to the community.

"You have this amazing gift, Ari," said Joan. "And we can use that gift to help other people."

"I like that idea, Mom, but how?"

Ariana really admired her mother. Joan might be the CEO of a company, but somehow she always found time to do things for her family, as well as other people.

"We're going to start a singing troupe and perform at events to raise money for charity," proclaimed her mum. "We'll call ourselves Kids Who Care."

Joan got about eight children together to rehearse, including Ariana and Aaron, and began organising performances at parties, weddings and bar mitzvahs. These small events were great experience for Kids Who Care, and Ariana became totally at ease with performing in front of all kinds of people.

Ariana continued to get parts with the local youth theatre, too. Playing Dorothy in *The Wizard of Oz* was a highlight of those years. Ariana had loved the film since she was four, so getting to wear the red shoes and sing 'Somewhere Over the Rainbow' was the fulfilment of a childhood dream.

"That song was made for you, *bellissima*," said her grandfather.

After that, there was a part in *Beauty and the Beast*. Ariana may have been small for her age, but whenever she stepped out onstage, she seemed to fill it with her presence...

Behind the scenes, Ariana was experimenting with making music of her own. Up in the music studio at home, she'd discovered the wonders of composing music on the computer. One of her great inspirations was a singer and musician called Imogen Heap. Like a sonic sorcerer, this English woman would layer recordings of her voice, then add other sounds, to create the most innovative songs Ariana had ever heard.

"Listen to that..." she told Frankie. Ariana was spellbound. "Her music is magical!"

Ariana tried to conjure her own musical magic,

using her voice, keyboards and the computer.

"What do you think of this?" she asked her brother as she played him her first ever composition. She'd named it 'Rain' and it was about – well, rain.

"Yeah." Frankie looked pleasantly surprised, because his sister was still only ten. "I like it!"

Ariana was thrilled. If her big brother approved, then she knew she'd hit the right note!

CHAPTER 8

THE BIG BREAK

"One day that girl is going to be a star."

So said Dennis Lambert, who lived next door to Ariana and just happened to be a music producer. He'd also co-written a heap of number-one hit songs in the 70s, so he knew his stuff.

Over the past summer, Lambert's daughter, Misha, had become Ariana's new best friend. Now that the girls were almost teenagers, they were always off on girly adventures together – to the beach, or searching through the racks at their favourite stores for hours, just to find the perfect top!

"Ariana's so funny, Dad," Misha told him. "She can imitate the sounds of all the dinosaurs in

Jurassic Park. I think she could be a brilliant comedian or comic actor, one day."

"Maybe, but it's her incredible singing voice that will get her to the top," Dennis predicted. "I've never heard a twelve-year-old sing like that before."

"Can you help her, Dad?" Misha was excited at the prospect.

"Well, I reckon Joan has it all under control," said Dennis. "Getting to the top is no easy business. But not letting success go to your head is the hardest thing of all – those two seem to have it sorted."

Ariana wasn't exactly 'sorted', but she knew which direction she wanted her career to take – for her, it was music all the way. She kept on doing her thing in the studio, coming up with new sounds and producing her voice in different ways. If she wasn't mistaken, she could reach the notes of a soprano; though she didn't really know, because she'd still not had any formal singing lessons.

The next major opportunity to come her way wasn't in music but in television, for a pilot TV show called *E-Venture Kids*, produced by a television company based in Boca Raton. Sadly for Ariana, the pre-teen educational programme was never shown. However, Ariana loved the experience and she got to work with her friend Aaron, so it had been a great laugh, too.

Things seemed to go her way when Joan secured a meeting with a music management company in Los Angeles.

"Right, Frankie," Ariana said – she was determined. "This is going to be *it* – I'm going to be signed up and then I'm going to make my debut album. Just you wait and see!"

"Ari, you've only just become a teenager," Frankie reasoned. "Slow down, don't get too excited. I don't want you to be disappointed. The music industry is a tough nut to crack." As ever, Frankie was being protective of his little sister.

"You know how much I love soul music," she went on. "It's my passion. Perhaps I was a soul singer in another life."

"Aww, little sis," laughed Frankie. "You have a beautiful voice, but I don't think you're ready yet."

"I am, I am!' insisted Ariana. "I'm going to make an R&B album, just like India Arie..."

The guys from Los Angeles were impressed with Ariana's voice. But, like Frankie had predicted, they just didn't think a fourteen-year-old could make a successful R&B album. Soul music was all about expression, and that came from experience. How could this young girl from Boca Raton, with her fine life and fancy background, have discovered the secret of soul music? They were not convinced.

However, Ariana was not put off. And then, as luck would have it, in came another offer...

"Wow, Ari – this is a big opportunity." Joan was fizzing with excitement as she put down the phone. Ariana flung herself into her mum's arms and waited for the news.

"What is it?" Ari's eyes were wide, brimming with excitement.

"It's a musical called *13* – have you heard of it?"

Ariana hadn't heard of it, because it was a brand-new musical, written by theatrical composer Jason Robert Brown. A few of his plays had made it to Broadway – the famous theatre strip in New York.

The play had opened in Los Angeles, but they were now casting for New York. The musical, *13*, was about a teenage boy whose parents get divorced and he moves from New York to a small town in Indiana. At his new school, he has to choose between the cool kids and the not-so-cool kids. The plot was great – Ariana identified with so much of it, as it chimed with things going on in her own life.

The music was fantastic, too – it was so modern and relevant. Songs like 'A Little More Homework' and 'It Can't Be True' would be fun to perform, and *so* different from anything she'd done before.

"Can you imagine working with a bunch of kids your own age?" Joan asked.

"That would be dreamy!" Ariana was goo-goo eyed at the very thought of it. "Mom, I've just *got* to get a part."

Aaron and Ariana headed to New York for the read throughs for the play. Aaron had also got a call from the theatrical agents, and the pair of them were ecstatic but extremely nervous. As Ariana sat in the waiting room to audition for *13*, she could feel her stomach doing somersaults. She hoped her trembling insides wouldn't stop her from doing a good reading.

Of course, she wanted the main female part – who wouldn't? – but she'd be happy with anything. Really!

"Really?" Ariana giggled nervously as she was handed a script. "You want me to read the granny part?"

Ariana was actually OK with this. She was a brilliant mimic. So she simply pretended she was one of Nonna's friends. It must have been good, because the casting directors were laughing.

After that, Ariana was told she had to get up to the microphone and deliver one of the show's rap songs.

"Cool!" Ariana's face lit up. "I love rapping!"

And she did. So she nailed it. The casting crew looked at each other in astonishment. This young girl from Florida certainly had 'it' – and she had buckets of energy.

"So, Aaron, what part did you get?" Ariana called up her friend as soon as she'd found out who she was playing.

"I'm Archie." Aaron was delighted to play Archie, a disabled kid, in the play.

Ariana was thrilled with her part, too. "Well, I'm Charlotte – you know, the cheerleader?"

"That's fantastic, Ariana," he said. "I'm so pleased for you!"

"Thanks," she said. "I know it's not the lead part, but I'm not ready for that yet – at least, not on Broadway!" And she meant it.

The whole gig was like a dream come true, but getting to work with Aaron was like the sprinkles on top of the icing on top of the gooiest, most delicious chocolate cake you could possibly imagine...

"Here's to you, Ari." The whole family were raising a glass to her as they sat around the dining table at home. Tomorrow she was off to Connecticut, to make her debut in *13*.

"Break a leg, little sister," said Frankie, who knew that the worst thing you could do in show business was to wish someone 'good luck'.

"You're on your way, little one," added Grande. "No one is going to stop you now."

"I've made your favourite," said Nonna as she plonked the big bowl of pasta with marinara sauce down in the middle of the table.

Everyone dived in with gusto.

"I'm going to miss you so much." Ariana shovelled

a spoonful of the yummy pasta into her mouth. "Especially your cooking, Nonna!"

The family burst out laughing.

CHAPTER 9

NEW YORK, NEW YORK

The play *13* kicked off at the Norma Terris Theatre in Chester, Connecticut in May 2008. Later that year, it opened on Broadway in New York, at the Bernard B. Jacobs Theatre.

The hustle and bustle of the big city didn't faze Ariana one bit. When she looked up at the towering skyscrapers of New York City, she felt exhilarated. She'd visited New York and seen countless musicals on Broadway since she was small – to be truthful, it felt a little bit like her second home. Now she was back again, but this time she was going to be in a musical on Broadway – her first professional job!

Just being in the city made Ariana feel like Holly Golightly, the heroine from her most adored film, *Breakfast at Tiffany's*. The character was played by one of her favourite actresses, Audrey Hepburn – Ariana had her poster on her bedroom wall at home. Ariana dreamed of being like Holly and finding happiness in New York...

Ariana was lucky to have her mum and Frankie with her in New York. Frankie had his own work commitments in the city and was always off for another audition, or performing. Joan rented an apartment for the three of them – she wanted to be there for both of her children. Not that Ariana felt like a child any more; she'd been thrust from middle school in Boca Raton to Broadway, but it felt normal to her. She was a big girl now and she was ready for whatever this great big city had to throw at her!

"Wow, my calves are burning," Ariana said as she rubbed her legs one evening. She was in love with what she was doing but it came at a price. "I mean, we've been on our feet for over twelve hours!"

The cast had just come offstage after another performance. Tonight, the crowd had been on their feet at the end, clapping like crazy. The sound of their applause was still echoing in Ariana's ears. She felt as high as a kite, but her legs hurt so much...

"I ache everywhere," exclaimed Aaron. "Even my eyebrows hurt!"

Ariana laughed at his joke.

"I'm so pleased we get to share this magic together," she added. "We've certainly moved on from Harry and Hermione!"

"I solemnly swear we are up to something good," quipped Aaron, who could recite *Harry Potter* at the drop of a sorting hat.

Ariana and Aaron were having the best time ever. The entire cast of *13* were teenagers and some days it just felt like one long party with your friends. Ariana got on really well with everyone, but especially Elizabeth Gillies, with whom she sang 'It Can't Be True'.

Elizabeth was making her professional debut, too, and it wasn't long before the girls were new BFFs – 'Best Friends Forever'. They shared a dressing room, and between rehearsals and performances they loved just hanging out together. Most of that time was spent larking around on their phones – taking selfies or recording pranks.

"Pass that magic potion, please," begged Ariana, who desperately wanted some ointment to soothe her poor aching muscles. "Tiger Balm doesn't do the trick any more."

"Here you go, Ari." Elizabeth threw the tube for Ariana to catch. "Then let's go and get a real ice cream. How about we go to Eddie's Sweet Shop for a sundae?"

"Aww, yum, let's do it!" Ariana bounced up enthusiastically. "Let's tell everyone!"

Hanging out with the cast and crew of *13* was always fun – practically everything about the whole acting experience was amazing. The only downside was the aches and blisters, but in a funny kind of way those niggly pains made you feel like a real professional!

13 went down in history, because it was the first musical with an all-teenage cast to play on Broadway. It opened on 5 October, 2008 and ran for 105 performances and 22 previews. Although she wasn't one of the main stars, Ariana stood out for her powerful voice, radiant smiles and sharp dance moves. She had a wonderful time and it showed in her performance.

The musical got fabulous reviews in the newspapers.

"Wow, the *New York Times* loves us!" exclaimed Aaron. "Apparently, we have 'radioactive energy'."

"Listen to this one in the *New York Theater*." Ariana read from the paper. "'*Mini-diva* Elizabeth Egan Gillies... is the cast member most likely to go on to Disney Channel fame.'"

"Yeah!" Elizabeth burst out laughing. "That's great to hear. But I reckon we'll all be on the Disney Channel one day – or Nickelodeon."

Ariana read all these reviews with interest, but she didn't take too much notice – she didn't let them go to her head and she was pleased for the kids who were praised. In her family, you were told to have faith in yourself, no matter what. You were also told to work hard. Ariana knew she could sing well and she had the drive to succeed.

The following year, *13* won a National Youth

Theatre Association Award and the cast celebrated together again. By this time, they were all going their separate ways and Ariana was on course for something new...

CHAPTER 10

DREAMS REALLY DO COME TRUE

In New York, Ariana auditioned for many roles. Like all actors, she got rejected time and time again. Sometimes it felt desperate, but Joan and Frankie were always there to support Ariana and keep her focused.

"Darling, don't worry," Joan reassured her after another disastrous audition. "You wait – something will work out. Right now, you have to get back up and keep trying."

"I know, Mom." Ariana looked at her mother with sad eyes. "It's no good taking it personally. Where will that get me?"

It was hard *not* take it to heart when she didn't get the parts, but the audition that day had been particularly tough. Ariana felt she had learned the songs and all the dance moves to perfection. At the audition, they seemed impressed and she really felt she had a chance. But then she got the tap on the shoulder and was told to leave the audition. Her heart sank.

"You just weren't silly enough," the director told her.

Ariana felt crushed – not silly enough? If anyone could do silly, she could! She would have loved to go back and show them just how goofy this Grande girl could be... But by the time she got home that night, she'd stopped fretting about it. It wasn't exactly her dream role, and there were many more auditions.

Ariana's dream role – the one that she went to bed thinking about, over and over – was Elphaba in *Wicked*. She loved the music and could imagine belting out all those amazing songs onstage. And the idea of playing the Wicked Witch of the West really appealed to her dark side and fascination with horror.

She never did get to audition for *Wicked*, but while she was still playing in *13*, Ariana was called back for several auditions for a new Nickelodeon series.

"I can't believe it," Ariana told Elizabeth Gillies. "Nickelodeon, no less!"

"We grew up watching that channel," said Elizabeth, who had also been asked to audition

"What do you mean? I still watch it. *iCarly* is, like, the best thing on TV at the moment!" Ariana was practically jumping round the room with excitement. The man behind *iCarly* was called Dan Schneider. Now, he was creating a brand-new teen sitcom, and he wanted to see Ariana and Elizabeth – it was jump-for-joy time!

A short while later, the girls were invited to LA. to do a screen test for the mysterious new series. It was incredible news, but the girls shared a doubt or two...

"I'm not sure about doing TV," Ariana confided in Liz one day, in their dressing room at the theatre.

"I know what you mean," Liz agreed. "I love performing live. It's in the moment, and you never really know what will happen next."

"Mmm. I can't imagine what it'd like to be

doing the same thing over and over in front of the cameras," Ariana went on. "And I'd miss the audience. TV is like another world..."

TV *was* another world, and so were the Nickelodeon studios on Sunset Boulevard in LA. At the studio, the girls were told a little more about the project. When they found out it was going to be a sitcom set in a performing arts high school, the girls flashed each other an excited look.

Neither of them attended high school any more. These days, Ariana had schoolwork sent up to her in New York from Florida. However, their time on *13* and other acting jobs had given them plenty of experience of the performing arts world. They both felt more than qualified for roles set in a cool performing arts high school!

On the way back to New York, the girls chattered non-stop about what would happen if they got roles.

"I'd move to LA – just like that," said Liz, clicking her fingers. "It'd be a dream come true."

"I know," Ariana agreed.

But deep inside she hardly dared dream that

she'd land the part. Imagine that – moving to Hollywood, the place where stars were born... it was just too much to hope for.

"Let's not get too excited yet, Liz. You know how it goes."

"Ariana!"

Frankie had picked up her phone, because she was way too nervous to answer.

"It's Dan Schneider here."

Ariana already knew that – his name had flashed up on the screen when the phone began ringing. She slowly took the phone. Her heart was beating double time...

"So, Ariana." Dan Schneider – *the* Dan Schneider – was speaking to her. "We were very impressed with your auditions. We thought you had amazing comedy timing and a real quirky way about you – you really made us laugh!"

"Th-thanks." Ariana's voice wobbled. "That's very kind."

"We've been looking for the right people to play the schoolkids in my new series."

"Mm-hmm..."

"We already have our protagonist. Remember Victoria who played Lola from *Zoey 101*? Well, she's the main character. But she's got loads of friends. Including this kooky character, Cat Valentine.

"And in New York, we thought you'd be the perfect girl to play Cat."

Ariana's heart skipped a beat.

"Then, when you came over to do a screen test for us in LA, we *knew* we'd found *the* perfect girl."

Ariana gulped.

"Say something, Ariana," laughed Dan. "I'm offering you the part of Cat. What do you think?"

What did Ariana think? She could hardly think, because her head was doing cartwheels and her heart was doing backflips!

Ariana had spent so much of her time wishing for parts in Broadway musicals, dreaming of being Elphaba or imagining herself releasing an album of R&B hits, that she'd never really considered that her next break would be in television. And she'd never dreamed she'd be plucked straight from the boards of Broadway to star in a brand-new series for Nickelodeon. Nonna had always told her "to expect the unexpected", and now that it was actually happening to her, she was flying!

CHAPTER 11

FEELING VICTORIOUS

Victorious began filming at the Nickelodeon Studios in LA in October 2009.

Ariana felt at home from the get-go! Best of all, Elizabeth had got a part, too. Their dressing room was enormous compared to the one at the theatre in Broadway – they had their own sofa and TV now. However, the place they loved to crash was the green room. It was *lush*, with its dim lighting, white leather sofas, big screens, video games and its own canteen – all in all, it was the perfect hangout for a gang of teenagers.

The green room was where the cast met and got to know one another better. Ariana was playing happy-go-lucky, scatty and chatty Cat Valentine.

Elizabeth had been cast as angry bad girl, Jade. Victoria Justice had the starring role, playing the talented and popular Tori Vega, who lands a place at a performing arts high school called Hollywood Arts. Avan Jogia was Jade's flirty boyfriend, Beck. Leon Thomas III played the musical genius Andre. Then there was Matt Bennett as geeky Robbie – the one who never went anywhere without his ventriloquist's dummy.

As soon as they started working together, Ariana had a good feeling – the cast just clicked and became friends in real life, too.

It was Dan Schneider who suggested that Ariana have her hair dyed red for the part of Cat.

As usual, Ariana asked Joan for her opinion.

"What do you think, Mom?"

"Well, it'll look cute, I guess," Joan said. "But I hope it doesn't make your hair fall out!"

Ariana had beautiful, long brown hair, but in the end she went with Dan's suggestion.

"Cat loves red-velvet cupcakes," Ariana reasoned. "So her hair should match her favourite cupcakes."

Cat Valentine really was completely bonkers and Ariana was enjoying getting into character.

It was funny how a change of hair colour could make you feel so different.

"I already feel fluffy, floaty and really... red!" Ariana said as she admired her new hair in the mirror.

After that, Ariana was shown the wardrobe department, where they kept racks of clothes for each character. Cat's clothes were ditzy, girly clothes in an array of pink, purple and brighter-than-bright colours.

"Mmm." Ariana put on a cute little skater dress and did a twirl. "I'm getting the idea..."

Next, she was given a cuddly purple giraffe to hold.

"He's so squishy and lovely!" Ariana looked at herself in the mirror and laughed – a lovely, throaty "Ha ha ha" that made other people in the wardrobe department want to laugh, too.

Ariana's transformation to Cat Valentine was nearly complete. Now, she had to dig deep and become Cat for the cameras – could she do it?

Ariana soon discovered that making television programmes was *very* different from being onstage. Between October 2009 and April 2010, she made twenty episodes for Season One of *Victorious*. Often, Ariana worked seven days a week. The schedule was absolutely frantic.

On Mondays and Tuesdays, Ariana would be in the studio, rehearsing with the rest of the cast. In the pilot, Cat had a line – "What's that supposed to mean?" – that would become her catchphrase, and it always got them all giggling.

On Wednesdays, Thursdays, Fridays and sometimes on Saturdays, too, they were filming. Ariana got up very early to go to hair and make-up, then she'd be on set all day, until very late at night sometimes. It was always exciting when the cameras were rolling and she got to say her lines for real. And, when everyone laughed, she knew that she'd nailed Cat Valentine!

On Sundays, Ariana had a few hours off. She loved living in LA and would have liked to explore her new neighbourhood, but time was precious. So when she had spare time, Ariana went back to doing what made her happiest – making music!

On Sunday nights, Ariana got the script for the next week. Often, she'd read it through with Frankie, who'd moved to LA, too. Cat's lines were usually kooky and Ariana had such a dreamy, not-quite-with-it way of delivering them that made them both laugh hysterically.

In March 2010, the cast of *Victorious* were invited to the famous Kids' Choice Awards. The Nickelodeon ceremony is held each year and attracts lots of famous stars. Ariana and the rest of the *Victorious* crew were beyond excited!

All the girls shared a hotel room, so they could get ready for the big night together. When they hit the red carpet, they looked so glamorous that people would never have guessed they'd been up most of the night having a girly sleepover. *Victorious* didn't win awards that year, because it hadn't aired yet, but the cast experienced their first red carpet event and it was totally exciting.

The pilot episode of *Victorious* aired on US television soon after the Kids' Choice Awards. It was love at first sight for many fans and the first series got some great reviews. Even though Tori was the star of the show, many viewers had a soft spot for Cat. She not only made them laugh, but in the episode 'Freak the Freak Out', she sang a duet with Jade, which blew them away. Nobody expected Cat to sing like that – it was the first sign that the little girl from Boca Raton was destined for even bigger things!

CHAPTER 12

WELCOME TO THE 'CITY OF ANGELS'

Becoming Cat Valentine was Ariana's ticket to a new life in LA – the 'City of Angels' in California. Ariana was enjoying her new life out west in sunny LA, but dealing with fame was another game. Like many young people, Ariana had taken to new social media – especially Twitter and Instagram. Fans of *Victorious* could follow her on a daily basis and she could respond to their tweets. Ariana soon developed a lovely relationship with many of her fans – in time, her avid bunch of followers would be called Arianators!

However, Ariana had never expected to be recognised out in public. Suddenly, a quiet meal with family and friends wasn't always possible.

Sometimes, if just one person realised they had 'Cat Valentine' sitting at the table next to them, within minutes the whole place knew.

People either piled over for an autograph, sat staring at her from behind a menu or carried on with their own meal, trying to pretend that they hadn't noticed her – it was all a bit bewildering but kind of cool!

Ariana had moved into a new home in LA with Joan and Frankie. This was a house with history, as it once belonged to a famous film director called Francis Ford Coppola. He'd made a film about an Italian family of gangsters, called *The Godfather*, and the first screening of this classic movie had taken place in the room that was now Ariana's bedroom.

"I'm not really a party girl – I'd rather be here, reading *Harry Potter* books," Ariana told the reporters who had come to film the rising star of *Victorious*.

Next, Ariana showed them her bedroom, where there were racks of fabulous shoes and a poster of film legend Marilyn Monroe. Ariana giggled and stated the obvious.

"I love shoes!"

Afterwards, she showed them the music room and introduced them to the wonders of her looping machine.

"Look! I can make harmonies on this and do weird things with my voice."

She demonstrated some of her vocal gymnastics.

"I play piano up here and sing, too." Ariana grabbed the microphone, opened her mouth and filled the room with her dynamic voice – just like that. The crew were taken aback – Cat Valentine was supposed to be a comic actress, not a singing sensation!

After that, Ariana showed the reporters her favourite room: the kitchen.

"I don't get much of a chance to cook," she explained. "Occasionally, I make lemon meringue pie for Frankie and me, and I use the lemons from our garden."

She showed them a gorgeous plump lemon she'd just picked.

"The swimming pool is over there." She pointed at the luxury pool. "I haven't been in it since I moved here over a year ago – that's how busy I am."

However busy and famous Ariana was becoming, she was just the same young girl she'd always been – she still had a fascination with creepy stuff.

"Ooh, Frankie and I call this the 'vampire dining room'." Ariana showed the reporters the wood-panelled room with a long table and high-back chairs. "Spooky, isn't it?" she said with a mischievous glint in her enormous eyes.

"Sometimes at night I hear strange noises and I think they're coming from in here..." Ariana actually looked delighted at this idea.

Finally, she showed them the basement – dark and filled with suitcases, it really did look a bit scary!

At seventeen, Ariana was living a life that many teenagers will only ever dream about. Deep inside, though, Ariana hadn't fulfilled her dreams yet. The desire to pursue her music just grew and grew – that was where her future lay. Tinkering in the home studio would occupy her for hours!

And Ariana did get to record music on the debut soundtrack for *Victorious*. Most of the songs on the album were sung by the lead actress in the series, Victoria Justice. The rest of the cast did their bit too, but 'Give it Up' was Ariana Grande and Elizabeth Gillie's number. Fans of the show had loved it when they heard it in the show, and it sounded even better on the compilation.

No one could deny that Ariana had tons of talent, but she realised that to get to the next level she would need some help. In stepped Katy Perry's vocal coach, Eric Vetro, who worked with Ariana on her vocal range. He showed her exercises to help her to perfect her skills, and encouraged her to practise over and over – something Ariana was always more than happy to do.

Christmas that year was a time of celebration for the family. In such a short time, Ariana had become a teen idol. Meanwhile, she was busily recording songs – maybe, just maybe, she'd get enough material together to make an album this year...

"Happy Christmas, everyone," Ariana beamed.

Around the room, were the people whom she loved most in the world and the ones who'd had been there for her as she followed her dreams.

"I have a little something for you, darling." Frankie handed Ariana a gift.

"Oh, you," Ariana said as she ripped off the wrapping. "You've already given me so much..."

"Aww, *bellissima*," gasped her grandfather. "It's an even tinier version of you – if that's possible!"

Everyone laughed as Ariana held up the plastic doll version of Cat Valentine.

"What's that supposed to mean?" quipped Ariana in her floaty Cat Valentine voice.

CHAPTER 13

BOLT OF INSPIRATION

'What's that supposed to mean?'

Cat's catchphrase was one of the many things that fans loved about *Victorious*. The show's popularity also meant that throughout 2011, Ariana and the cast were busily filming Season Two.

Playing Cat Valentine was wonderful, but Ariana knew there was something else she was destined to do. As she watched the crowd going berserk at a Katy Perry concert, Ariana knew exactly where she wanted to be.

"She's amazing, Frankie."

Ariana jumped up and down – it wasn't easy seeing over the heads of everyone, trying to get a glimpse of the mighty Katy Perry onstage, when you're only five foot tall.

"Your first ever concert, little sister." Frankie smiled. "You never forget your first concert!"

And Ariana never did forget it, especially when she heard Katy Perry sing her hit, 'Firework'. The crowd knew every word of the song – it clearly meant a lot to them. That night, Ariana witnessed the power of song. She also saw a great diva in action. Ariana felt another bolt of inspiration coursing through her body – Grandpa was right all along. Getting up onstage, like Katy, and performing in front of thousands of fans was what she was destined to do...

How do you become a megastar? Justin Bieber had done it through YouTube. His mother had uploaded videos of her boy singing, to share with friends and family. Word got around and, before they knew it, the videos attracted thousands of followers.

Ariana loved to film herself singing – she'd done it since she was a little girl. All those videos with her friends and Frankie had been building towards something. Now, she started making videos to share with the whole world. She began with Adele's 'Rolling in the Deep', and moved on to covers of Mariah Carey and Whitney. At the time, Ariana had no idea who would watch her videos, but she hoped that the faithful Cat Valentine fans would follow her. Whatever happened, it sure felt right putting her music out there.

And so it was through the power of YouTube that Ariana was discovered. Monte Lipman of Republic Records had been told by a friend to watch this young singer online. Immediately, Monte was struck by the young woman's immense talent and passion. He recognised that rare thing they call 'star quality' – Ariana had it in bucketloads. From there, things moved quickly – Monte called Ariana up for a meeting.

"You're already a star of a TV show," Monte told her. "But I reckon you are destined for even bigger things."

Ariana's first single, 'Put Your Hearts Up', was recorded swiftly and was released in time for Christmas. Ariana was delighted with the 1960s sound and the message of the song.

"It's a song that I hope inspires people to open

their hearts up," she said, "and realise that even the smallest acts of kindness can make the world a better place."

Making the video for 'Put Your Hearts Up' was like making her own mini movie.

"Ooh, I feel so nervous," admitted Ariana to her mother. "It's just me in front of the camera – I miss my *Victorious* gang!"

"You'll be wonderful, Ari," Joan reassured her daughter, who was wearing a glorious pink dress and looked sensational despite her nerves.

"There's no one to have a laugh with," she explained. "I hope I can do it."

Ariana didn't need to worry; she was a natural. From the opening scene, where she released a cartoon butterfly, to the bridge scene, which reminded her of her favourite classic movies, she looked happy and carefree. The video was like a fantasy world and Ariana felt like Audrey Hepburn twirling through a dream!

Ariana didn't forget her fans in all of this. She posted four possible covers for the single on her Twitter account and the fans voted for their favourite. This was new territory for the record company, but for Ariana this relationship with her fans through social media was as easy as 1-2-3.

'Put your Hearts Up' didn't make number one in the charts. In fact, it didn't make the charts, but Ariana's career as a recording artist had started.

At the age of eighteen, life was pulling Ariana in many directions. Her heart was bursting with joy, because she was making records and starring in gorgeous videos. However, she loved being on the set of *Victorious* with her gang of co-stars. In only a few years, Ariana's life had transformed. What would be next?

CHAPTER 14

SAM, CAT AND SNOW WHITE, TOO

The cast of *Victorious* had to wait until 2012 before they won the Kids' Choice Award for Favourite TV Show. The ceremony was a night to remember. It was hosted by Will Smith, and the presenters included the president's wife, Michelle Obama, as well as Zac Efron and Nicki Minaj. Ariana couldn't believe how far she had come. She was a massive Nicki Minaj fan and now they were sharing the same stage!

Although she enjoyed red-carpet events, Ariana wasn't a party girl at heart. A night spent at home, eating her favourite sushi or playing video games, was much more her thing. And, back at her house, she could always shuffle off to the studio and spend hours writing songs, mixing music and playing around with vocal effects. The album was a way off yet, but she gave it the working title *Daydreamin'*. Ariana was the queen of daydreaming, but she was also the master of making dreams comes true!

As she turned nineteen, Ariana was filming the third series of *Victorious* and seemed happy about the way things were going.

"So what does 2012 hold for you, Ariana?" asked one reporter visiting the set of *Victorious*.

"You know I love working on *Victorious*, I really do. So expect lots more silliness from Cat." She laughed. "And maybe an album!"

"So is that where your career is headed?" the reporter probed.

"I'm not sure," she answered. "But I hope for the rest of my life that I am lucky enough to be doing what I'm doing now: acting, singing and performing. I'm incredibly lucky and I do not take a single moment for granted."

Ariana was enjoying everything that was happening, but a few months later things changed again.

"I can't believe it's ending, Nonna." Ariana was shivering, despite the hot August sun – sometimes emotions got her that way. "*Victorious* is being axed."

"Oh, you're going to miss those friends you've made, aren't you, darling?" Nonna said.

"We've been through so much together," Ariana sobbed. "None of us want it to be over."

"There, there, honey." Nonna searched for something to say. "Remember – when something ends, something new can begin."

"I know... but we have such chemistry together."

"Ahh, you lot will stay friends for ever!" Nonna hugged Ari close.

"Yes." Ariana was crying and laughing now. "They've not seen the last of me. We'll be friends until we're about 900 years old!"

The world had not seen the last of Cat Valentine, either. Dan Schneider had other ideas for the kooky character. He'd been dreaming up another teen comedy, but this time starring Cat Valentine from *Victorious* and Sam Puckett from *iCarly*. Jennette, who played Sam, had already met Ariana at Nickelodeon events and

Dan had noticed there was a certain chemistry between the girls that he felt would work well on screen.

"I can't believe we're doing this *Sam and Cat* thing – whatever it is..." Ariana told Jennette one day when they met up for milkshakes.

"Me neither, Ari!" Jennette slurped her shake.

Ariana giggled. Jennette was as funny in the flesh as she was on screen. *Sam and Cat* was going to be enormous fun – whatever it was!

The story of *Sam and Cat* began with Sam rescuing Cat from the back of a garbage truck and the girls becoming friends and then room-mates. This led to Cat's wacky idea of them starting up a babysitting business called Sam & Cat's Super Rockin' Fun-Time Babysitting Service.

"Just imagine the madness that we can squeeze from this plot," said Dan excitedly.

"Wow." Ariana liked the idea. "It's a great opportunity for us, too."

"Yep, it's cool," agreed Jennette, looking over at Ariana with a smile.

The girls were fast becoming good friends – a big bonus if you're working together for over sixteen hours a day!

Friendship was important to Ariana, who always described the cast of *Victorious* as family. They just couldn't get enough of one another – if they weren't filming the show then they were uploading their own comedy sketches to their YouTube channel, 'Stoop Kid'.

The cast were invited to Ariana's nineteenth birthday in June. In September, when Team *Victorious* arrived at the Creative Arts Emmys, they were still laughing and joking together. Ariana told a journalist: "These are my favourite people ever. I laughed the hardest I've ever laughed with these guys." *Victorious* had ended, but the friendships lived on.

Christmas was a special time of year for Ariana, and that year she got to spend the run-up to the festive period at the Pasadena Playhouse in California, playing Snow White. This new production was a bit like a traditional English pantomime but with lots of modern songs by the likes of Katy Perry and Bruno Mars. It was funny and the audience was encouraged to join in! Ariana often found herself laughing too, but she managed to rein in that infectious laugh to sing a beautiful version of Katy Perry's 'Firework'. Slowed down and given the power-ballad treatment, Ariana made 'Firework' her own, up on the stage at Pasadena.

"Yay!"

Ariana was in the dressing room, getting ready for a performance.

"It feels so good to be brunette again!"

Dyeing her hair red for the part of Cat Valentine had played havoc with Ariana's hair. It had started falling out in chunks and she'd had to style her hair carefully to hide those bald patches. Luckily, Dan had agreed she could wear a wig when she returned to filming early next year. For now, it was bliss to be back to normal.

"You really are the perfect Snow White."

Joan loved seeing her daughter dressed up like a princess – it took her back to Ariana's childhood, when Ariana was always dressing up as something.

"I love being back onstage, Mom." Ariana glowed with enthusiasm. "You know me, I'm never happier than when I'm performing!"

Ariana was also very happy when she was with her family, but lately there had been some sad news. Her beloved grandfather had been told he had cancer. Somehow, he still managed to fly to LA to see his little princess perform. Being professional and fulfilling your commitments was the Grande family code. The show must go on – and Ariana did her grandfather proud, as she played Snow White to packed audiences every night.

CHAPTER 15

MILLIONS OF MAGICAL MOMENTS

Juggling TV and music and performing onstage had become a way of life for Ariana. It was hard work, but she had inherited her grandparents' and parents' work ethic. In late 2012, that drive to create wonderful music was recognised by one of the most famous people in the music talent-management business. Scooter Braun was the man who had spotted the unknown Justin Bieber on the Internet and got him a record deal.

Now, he was knocking at Ariana Grande's door.

"If you sign with me, there's no going back." Scooter was charming but firm with her. "You must give it everything you have."

All eyes were on Ariana. Her mother and

Frankie were always there to support her when there were major opportunities to discuss. This felt like the biggest decision of her life.

"I'm ready." Ariana's face lit up with the biggest smile of her life. "But is the world ready for me?"

Ariana had been recording songs in her own recording studio at home for years. Her eye had always been on recording her own solo album. At fourteen, Ariana had wanted to make an album just like India Arie. Five years later, aged nineteen, she was *finally* ready to make that album – more than ready, she would say!

"Are you ready, Ariana?" The sound engineer looked over at Ariana, who was grinning on the outside and bursting with joy inside.

The atmosphere in the recording studio was electric. Ariana was just so happy to be there – finally, she was recording the vocals for her first single for her debut album, and it felt like magic!

'The Way' was a song about a relationship – the lyrics were flirty and fun and much more grown-up than her previous single. The sound was edgier, too, with samples of R&B that Ariana loved.

"This is the real me!" Ariana was excited by the new direction her music was taking, so when she sang the words, she meant them: "I love it, I love it..."

Later, rapper Mac Miller stepped up to record his bit. On a scale from one to ten, Ariana was at one hundred – just like in the song!

In February 2013, the final episode of *Victorious* was aired in the US. By then, Ariana was sporting the Cat Valentine red wig and filming the first series of *Sam and Cat*. Dan had been right – there were plenty of hilarious escapades for the girls in this new show. These BFF had to deal with some weird clients – from babysitting goats to looking after creepy dolls, nothing seemed beyond Sam and Cat's Super Rockin' Fun-Time Babysitting Service! Cat Valentine was well and truly back, and her fans were as devoted as ever...

That year, life sped up again – if that were possible. Recording her album had to be squeezed between everything else. If Ariana wasn't filming *Sam and Cat* then she was attending promotional events and doing countless interviews. Dressing up for the red carpet and being photographed by anyone who could get near her was fun yet draining.

"Smile for us, Ariana!" the photographers called out. She was a natural in front of the camera. Smiles came easily, but sometimes it was hard work – especially when she really wanted to be in the recording studio, completing her album.

In February, Ariana filmed the video for 'The Way', and it was time for another transformation. Cat Valentine was gone in an instant. In her place was Ariana Grande. Her natural brown hair was swept back, with a tumble of curls down her back. All those cute dresses were replaced with simple black and white clothes. Suddenly, she looked older and she was partying with Mac Miller and a crowd of urban kids in a room filled with balloons. The video even ended with a kiss with Mac...

In between her hectic schedule, Ariana kept up with her fans via Twitter, Instagram and YouTube. Nobody knew better than Ariana how to reach out to her fans and send them teasers about what she was up to. On 5 March, she tweeted about her new single, 'The Way'. Then, on 13 March, she announced the release date. There was a flurry of excitement for Arianators everywhere!

'The Way' was released on 25 March, 2013. At the time, Ariana felt she was looking for 'the way' in her own life. She'd hit a crossroads in her career.

"It's really hard to describe," said Ariana as she tried to explain to Frankie anyway. "I mean, I love playing Cat. Part of the reason for that is when I'm Cat Valentine I know it makes my young fans so happy." Everyone knew how much Ariana cared for her fans.

"*Sam and Cat* is such a hoot, Ari," Frankie agreed. "They do adore you."

"But I'm getting older, Frankie. I'm going to be twenty soon," she went on. "Perhaps it's my time to develop as a recording artist. Now I can make the kind of music I've always wanted to. It feels so amazing to be actually making my own urban pop, rather than listening to the old divas doing it."

"So what's the problem?" Frankie asked.

"Can I be Cat Valentine and Ariana Grande at the same time – is it too much?"

"If anyone can do it, you can, Ari."

"Are you ready, Ariana?"

Scooter and some of the management team were gathered in his office with Ariana. She nodded, because she just couldn't speak – today, nerves had got the better of her! The record had sold 120,000 units in the first two days of its release – that was epic. Now, they were waiting for the Billboard Hot 100 chart.

"*Yes*!" Ariana was jumping around the office as the chart rundown was announced. 'The Way' had reached number ten in its debut week. "I think that means they like it!"

"Well done, Ariana." Scooter gave her a hug. "There's no looking back now!"

In June, the first series of *Sam and Cat* was broadcast on US television. The show was watched by over four million viewers. Many of them were massive fans of Cat Valentine and Ariana Grande. In a few short years, Ariana had achieved incredible success.

The eager young girl from Boca Raton had blazed a trail of stardom. Now a confident teenager, she was watched by millions, her music was listened to by millions and she was followed by millions on social media.

Next, she wanted to release an album that sold millions of copies. With Scooter by her side, anything seemed possible...

CHAPTER 16

THE BREAKTHROUGH

What a rollercoaster-ride it was the year Ariana turned twenty. Ariana's life was still going superfast, hurtling towards stardom. Fame brought the media out in packs, and they wanted to know what made this little diva tick.

Of course, many of those journalists wanted to discover whether she preferred acting or singing.

"It's so hard to tell them what I really feel," she confided in her old friend Aaron. "I auditioned for *Victorious* because I thought it would help my singing career."

"Ahh, and you *are* a great actress," Aaron replied.

"I fell in love with playing Cat," Ariana admitted.

"But my gut instinct has always been that I'd be a singer. And, I reckon I understand music more."

"Are you considering giving up on Cat?" Aaron asked.

"I don't know." Ariana looked puzzled. "But I'm a *far* better singer than actress."

People often asked Ariana how fame had changed her life. Again, Ariana was upfront and honest, and explained how she missed just going out to ordinary places with no make-up and messy hair.

"Everywhere I go these days, I'm recognised," she told Elizabeth Gillies.

"It's more difficult for you, Ari, than it is for me," Elizabeth sympathised. "It's hard to escape Cat Valentine's shadow."

"It's not just that. People write about how I look all the time. They can be so mean and cruel. I can't even sneeze without somebody having an opinion. I just never expected it to be like this."

"You handle it all very well, though." Elizabeth tried to be supportive. The fame game wasn't always easy to play.

"Some days I'm at the TV studio until ten at

night," Ariana explained. "Then I rush home to meet a choreographer to practise dance moves until three in the morning. This is a full-time commitment!"

"Totally." Elizabeth smiled. "I'm not sure how you do it sometimes."

"Luckily for me, I have some brilliant friends." Ariana grinned at Elizabeth. "And an amazing family. Talking with you lot helps me to deal with it all."

Ariana also managed to keep on top of things because she looked after herself. As well as dancing and meditation, she worked out on her cross-trainer gym machine to her favourite music by Nicki Minaj and Bruno Mars. She loved delicious home-cooked food like pasta and puddings, as well as fresh fruit – pineapple, mango and strawberries were always on the shopping list! By the end of the year, Ariana posted on Twitter that she was a vegan, too.

That summer, Ariana's debut album was nearly ready to go and she was eager to tell people all about it. During interviews, Ariana talked about her musical heroes.

"Oh wow, I have so many influences," she told

the reporters. "Artists like Amy Winehouse and India Arie. But then I love 1950s girl bands like The Shirelles, too."

When people asked Ariana about her new album, she tried to describe how she did it.

"I've been as honest as I can be," she explained in interviews. "I've opened up my heart. It's almost like I've made music rather than kept a diary to record all my feelings."

The release date of the album was getting closer, but Ariana was very busy in the meantime.

"Look at my schedule, Mom." Ariana showed the planner on her phone to Joan. It appeared that every day for the next few months was fully booked up. "It's gone crazy!"

"Yes, you're certainly a busy young woman." Joan looked proud. "Let's see."

First, there was the Billboard Music Awards, then there was the release of Ariana's second single, 'Baby I', and all the promotions surrounding that...

"And that's just July, Mom!" Ariana looked excited. "August is awesome!"

Ariana was booked to play the opening slot on

Justin Bieber's closing concerts of his 'Believe' tour in early August before headlining her first solo tour called 'Listening Sessions'. Later in August, she was going to record a video with Nathan Sykes of the band The Wanted, and then, on 25 August, she was due to perform at the MTV Video Music Awards!

"But the thirtieth of August is the most truly awesome of all." Ariana's face shone with delight. "*Finally* I release *Yours Truly* – everything I've ever hoped and dreamed about is actually happening."

"You deserve it, Ariana, you've worked very, very hard." Joan hugged her close.

"I couldn't have done it without you, Mom. I love you so much."

At the beginning of September, *Yours Truly* debuted at number one on the Billboard 200 charts. The album was a chart success all around the world, reaching the top ten in the UK, Australia, Canada, Japan and beyond. Fans loved it, and so did the critics, who praised Ariana's voice, composition and lyrics. Ariana was delighted when *Entertainment Weekly* called it 'One of the most purely enjoyable albums of the year.'

"Yesss!" She punched the air as she read that one. "I've done it!"

Ariana was always grateful for her opportunities in life, and in November she got to say her thank yous at the American Music Awards. Wearing a red sparkling evening gown, Ariana tottered towards the stage a little unsteadily – she was totally used to wearing high heels, but tonight she felt *so* nervous. The winner of New Artist of the Year had just been announced – and it was her!

It was a massive, wonderful moment and Ariana was overcome with emotion.

"Oh my," she said as clutched the award. "I'm so nervous. Thank you so much. This is for my fans – I have the best fans in the world. I love them so much."

She now had about thirty seconds to thank all the people who'd helped her – it seemed an impossible task. She pulled out a list her mother had written for her and reeled off the names in double-quick time.

As ever, Ariana delivered in her own sweet style. And the crowd loved her even more.

CHAPTER 17

SINGING FOR THE PRESIDENT

The following year, Ariana turned twenty-one and began recording her second album. *Yours Truly* echoed Mariah Carey and all the other urban soul acts Ariana had grown up listening to.

She promised her next album would sound very different: "I don't want it to sound like an extension of *Yours Truly*. I want it to sound like an evolution. I want to explore more sounds and experiment a little bit. I have a bunch of ideas I'm very excited about and a lot of stuff cooking."

As ever, Ariana had lots of 'stuff cooking' outside the recording studio, too. She'd even been asked to perform for President Obama and Mrs Obama at the White House, alongside music legends like

Aretha Franklin. Stepping up on the stage just a few metres away from the president and his wife felt nerve-racking, but Ariana managed to sweeten her greeting.

"Mr President, Mrs Obama – what's up? How are you? Good to see you."

Ariana's natural charm made everyone, including the President, smile. And those smiles turned to applause as she powered her way through the Whitney Houston classic 'I Have Nothing,' and her own song 'Tattooed Heart'.

Ariana couldn't believe it when she was asked to perform for the Obamas again later that spring!

"Even though I've done it before, I'm still shaking all over."

"Don't worry," Joan said. "You'll shine."

Ariana was greeted by the warm smile of the President again as she performed on the south lawn of the White House for the annual Easter Egg Roll. That afternoon, Ariana performed her hits 'The Way' and 'Right There'. It was only after she'd finished her songs that Ariana finally stopped trembling – at least, for a little while.

Another guest that day was the actor Jim Carrey. He was Ariana's childhood crush, and meeting him in the flesh was both awesome and embarrassing all at the same time – Ariana's insides were in bits.

"Look, look, Mom – it's Jim Carrey!" Ariana began shaking again as the famous actor approached them. "I don't think I can even speak..."

"What, *you* not be able to talk?" Joan laughed. "Never."

But it was no joke. Jim was friendly and funny and everything Ariana ever hoped he'd be, but she could hardly say a word! Even so, meeting her teen idol was one of the happiest moments of her life.

And there was so much to be happy about in Ariana's life.

In April, she released her first single from the next album. 'Problem' had actually been a problematic song for Ariana. Somewhere in the recording studio she had fallen out of love with it and she had a gut feeling it wasn't the song she wanted to release first. Not even the addition of sassy Australian rapper Iggy Azalea and America's Big Sean made her feel totally convinced.

"I'm not sure this should even go on the album," she told Scooter.

Ariana needn't have worried – 'Problem' became her breakaway single, the one that catapulted her to the superstardom she'd always dreamed about. The song reached number two in the US and debuted at number one in the UK, Ireland, Scotland and New Zealand. It was a worldwide hit, and later in the year it scooped MTV awards for best pop video and song of 2014.

Life had been going at full speed, Ariana thought to herself, and now here she was – sat on a plane zooming through the night sky, going home to Florida. Despite her busy schedule, nobody could have stopped her from making this trip. Grandpa's cancer had got much worse. Ariana's lovely, amazing, funny Grande was very ill and she was flying home to say goodbye. She clutched a tissue in her hand. She'd already cried so much it felt like she had no more tears left to cry. Holding him for the last time was going to be one of the hardest things she ever did. It didn't seem that long ago that he was cuddling her and telling her she would be a star – that she was his little diva. If only they had longer...

Frank Grande passed away in July and Ariana was heartbroken. This time she used Twitter to thank her fans for their support.

"My fans really do bring me love and light," she explained to Joan. "They totally know how much I love my grandpa."

The blow of losing her grandfather had just hit, and then Ariana heard that *Sam and Cat* was going to be cancelled. She felt almost numb at the news – she sat looking into space, trying to make sense of it all. Yes, in one way she'd been struggling to juggle being both Cat Valentine and Ariana Grande. Yet, now she'd been told that she'd never play Cat again, she felt empty. She'd just loved playing alongside Jennette. They'd made thirty-five episodes together and had a total laugh.

But the hardest part of it all was saying farewell to her dear old friend Cat. She loved that red-haired, scatterbrained girl, too! Cat was positive and passionate. In a funny way,

Cat had seen Ariana grow from a teenager to a young woman. She'd always be thankful to her for that.

But now, it was time to go it alone – to go solo as Ariana Grande.

That summer, Ariana had celebrated her twenty-first birthday and graduated to the big-girl school of pop. British star Jessie J had invited Ariana and Nicki Minaj to join her on the track 'Bang Bang'. Ariana felt at ease with her feisty companions and added her own brand of girl power to the track. The song became one of the biggest summer tunes of 2014 and hit the number-one spot in both the UK and the US digital charts.

Throughout the summer months, Ariana released snippets of information about other songs that would feature on her album. Her Instagram followers got a taste of 'Best Mistake' and 'Love Me Harder', and Arianators waited patiently for the next release...

"Don't you ever need a break, little sister?" Frankie asked Ariana.

"Aww. I can always unwind in the studio," Ariana told him.

"Sure, you've always been able to do that – but don't you miss just hanging out at the beach sometimes?"

Ariana's face went a little dreamy as she thought about the waves crashing onto the shore at Boca Raton. And then she imagined the tropical heat that she loved so well. It was healing and helped her vocal cords to relax.

"Mmm, I guess so. A day just swimming and taking it easy... followed by Coconut Bliss ice cream. Mmm... and then just a cool evening snuggling with my friends, maybe playing Wii."
Ariana felt a jolt as she pulled herself back to reality. It did all sound so blissful, but for now it was head down and on with business.

CHAPTER 18

HERE COMES MY EVERYTHING

Ariana slid into the passenger seat of the car. She fished her phone from her bag and fiddled with its settings until it was paired with the audio system. Suddenly, the sound of her singing filled the car. The melodic introduction – simply called 'Intro' – of her brand-new album *My Everything* sounded awesome as it pumped through the car's speakers.

"This has always been my favourite way of listening to new songs!" Ariana turned to her mum with a grin. "I wanted to hear the album like this with you, before it's released..."

As they drove around, they listened to songs like 'One Last Time', 'Be My Baby', 'Love Me Harder' and 'Just a Little Bit of Your Heart' with big smiles on their faces. All the hard work had been completely worth it.

"I just wish Grande had heard it," said Ariana as they listened to the song 'My Everything'. This was the song she'd dedicated to him, so it would always have a special place in her heart. Silent tears slid down her face as the song came to its gentle end.

The evening of *My Everything*'s release was everything a pop princess could ever wish for, and more. It began on the red carpet at the 2014 MTV Video Music Awards. Ariana arrived with her grandma on her arm. The crowd whistled and called her name as she smiled towards them. That night, she looked sensational in a black leather dress with her signature ponytail swishing this way and that as she twirled and posed for the cameras.

There was another wardrobe change when she appeared onstage to perform 'Bang Bang' with Jessie J and Nicki Minaj. Wearing a black-and-white satin costume and strutting around the enormous stage, she looked a total star! Like partners in crime, the three pop stars stole the show.

But there was more to come – Ariana then pulled off an epic performance of 'Break Free'. She wowed the crowd as she stepped down from a space capsule wearing a sparkling pink outfit and thigh-high boots. All those after-hours choreography lessons had really paid off, as she moved with the dancers in perfect time. But, as ever, it was Ariana's sensational voice that made the crowd go wild. Everywhere Ariana looked there were hands waving in the air in time to the music. She skipped and whirled as her heart filled with joy.

The night could hardly get any better, but it did when Ariana heard her name announced as winner for the best pop video of the year with 'Problem'. Wow – her heart did flips and tricks as she stepped up to receive the award from none other than her childhood crush, Mr Jim Carey!

Ariana hadn't expected to win so hadn't prepared a speech. In true Ariana style, she thanked her fans first and told them how much she loved them. Finally, when she got backstage, Ariana burst into tears – tears of total and utter happiness.

After the show, Ariana was interviewed by the press. It was then she announced that her new album, *My Everything*, was being released in about an hour. When they asked her how she was going to celebrate, she told them she'd swing by her record company's party, but really she was just looking forward to going home to be with friends and family.

My Everything was another smash hit for Ariana. In its first week, it went to number one in the US, Australia and Canada, and made it to number three in the UK.

Ariana was pleased with the album and told *Billboard*: "I'm a perfectionist, so I never thought I'd be able to say this, but I love this album five times as much as *Yours Truly*. They're different, but I love this one so much more."

One of the hardest tasks any artist has to go through is reading reviews of their music and live performances. Katy Perry and Miley Cyrus had both warned Ariana not to take anything to heart – unless it was good, of course! – so she did her best to be positive. Ariana quickly scanned the reviews of *My*

Everything in the bundle of papers and magazines in front of her. *Yes!* she thought, *these are pretty much all amazing – something she could take to heart!* She lost no time and FaceTimed Frankie.

"Frankie, Frankie," she practically yelled into her phone. "*Rolling Stone*, repeat, *ROLLING STONE* magazine love it!"

"Hey, Ari, that's so cool!" Frankie shrieked back.

"Check this, they actually say 'There's no limit to where Ariana Grande can go from here'... They describe me as a 'major force'!"

Frankie laughed. "They got that right!"

"And, Frankie, listen to this one in Digital Spy." Ariana was glowing with delight. "*My Everything's* mixed bag proves that whatever the genre, Ariana's voice shines supreme. Believe the title – this is Ariana's everything, and she's taking it right to the top."

Ariana was at the top! And being in the limelight meant she was in demand on many famous American shows. On 29 August, a massive crowd gathered to see Ariana perform her hits in the

Today plaza, New York, for the *Today* show. After singing 'Problem', 'Break Free', 'Bang Bang' and 'Break Your Heart', Ariana went back to the studio to help with the weather forecast and did the 'happy dance' with Al, the *Today* weatherman. Ariana's grandmother turned up to be interviewed, too.

That was the day the *Today* show became *The Ariana Show* and Ariana proved that she really *was* top of her game.

CHAPTER 19

THE HONEYMOON

In 2015, Ariana set off on her first world tour. The 'Honeymoon' tour would take her across North America, over to Europe and Asia, and then to South America.

Ariana was ready for action. She'd worked out especially hard to get her lungs and breathing stronger. Vocal training was essential so that she didn't harm her voice when she used it every day on tour. Then there were all the choreography and dance moves to learn. Ariana was also hands-on with all the musical arrangements. She had her say in what the back-up singers would do, and helped arrange parts for the strings, horns and all the band. The 'Honeymoon' tour was Ariana's opportunity to show the world what she could do and she wanted to shine!

The tour kicked off in February, in Kansas City, Missouri and finished in Sao Paulo in South America in October. It was an epic nine months filled with travel, rehearsals, showtime, backstage fun, dramas – and dogs. Ariana took her furry entourage of rescue dogs everywhere she could and her cheeky hounds Toulouse and Sirius were the lucky ones this time! Once again, Ariana was surrounded by friends and family – Joan was there every step of the way, and Grandma and Frankie were there when they could be. All the members of the backstage team – from the dancers to the make-up artists – became like family within a short space of time and, just like those happy days on the set of *Victorious*, there was a party atmosphere behind the scenes. Before each show, all the singers, musicians and dancers would link arms with Ariana and Joan in a prayer circle, to give each other words of support and encouragement.

Ariana never forgot her fans: "Be loud," she'd implore them from behind the stage. "Show us your love. We hope you have the best night of your life!"

On the opening night in Kansas City, Ariana gave it all she had. The crowd was fizzing with excitement even before she'd made her entrance. Ariana burst onto the stage singing 'Bang Bang'. From there it was a high-octane mix of pumping music, slick dance routines, fabulous glittering costumes, bubble-gum pink lighting, soaring lasers, flashing fireworks, video interludes and sensational vocals (plus a few cat's ears!) from the one and only Ariana Grande and her exquisite troupe of dancers and musicians.

Fans savoured every moment, whether it was Ariana strutting and dancing energetically in a sparkling black outfit and killer heels as she delivered her hit 'Hands On Me', or sitting atop a white grand piano wearing a sensational skirt strewn with flowers, singing 'Pink Champagne' and 'Tattooed Heart'.

Next, there was 'One Last Time' and then she delighted the audience with her magical musical gloves as she sang 'Why Try'. Things became emotional with Ariana's tribute to her grandpa. Conversations they had were flashed up on the large screen.

"Music — you want to do something in music?" The voice of Frank Grande filled the auditorium.

"Go ahead and do it. Don't be afraid of it. There's so much music; you gotta work on it. Don't let them challenge you; don't let them intimidate you. Do your thing, that's the only way to do it."

It became clear where Ariana got her drive and determination from, and it sent shivers down many spines in the audience. Afterwards, Ariana sang 'My Everything' with tears in her eyes.

After that, Ariana left the stage for a short break. It was good to grab a few moments to catch her breath and steady her nerves. When 'Lovin' It' started up, that was her cue to get back on again. The next number was 'Love Me Harder' and she was going to perform it on a pedestal over the stage. While the dance crew threw themselves around the stage in another dynamic dance routine, Ariana was inside a lift taking her up to the pedestal.

"I just hate this thing," Ariana whispered in frustration as she couldn't get out of the lift. It was then she realised that the lift was broken and she was in danger of being crushed between wood and metal.

"Help!" Ariana tried not to panic but it was terrifying.

"Quick," one of the stage crew noticed the situation. "We're here."

Ariana clung on to a beam and somehow the crew got her to safety, where she could continue with the show. Nobody in the audience noticed the near disaster that night. Ariana just kept on singing and her fans were in raptures.

Nerves never got the better of Ariana, whatever happened on that all-shining and shimmering tour. Sometimes she tripped or fell. Other times she lost a shoe or hit a member of the crew by accident during a dance routine. She even fluffed her words or got the giggles.

Ariana often used the stage as a platform for telling people how she really felt. "Love your family. Cherish them," she told the crowd. And on another occasion she waved a gay pride flag and told her gay fans to "Come out in your own time, and remember I love you." Ariana's brother, Frankie, was gay, and she believed everyone had the right to love who they wanted.

Ariana always delighted in her fans' reaction to

the show. "I love you so much" was something she told her fans over and over again – onstage, through Twitter and Instagram, and on her YouTube channel called 'Honeymoon Diaries'. Some lucky fans even got to meet her in specially arranged meet-and-greets, where they had selfies and an opportunity to chat with the pop princess herself!

CHAPTER 20

LUCK. LOVE AND THE SECRET OF HAPPINESS

Being a pop princess was a serious business and Ariana had cracked it. Everywhere she went on the 'Honeymoon' tour, she was greeted by ecstatic fans wearing the cat ears that Ariana loved and flashing phone cameras in her direction. But guess what? Sometimes it actually became boring sitting in the back of a limousine, being whizzed from one place to another.

However, this was Paris, and Ariana was in a playful mood sitting in the back of the limo slurping a drink. Most people would be staring at the famous landmarks, but Ariana was having a blast with two boys on a motorbike. They'd spotted her sitting in the back of the car beside them and had called out to her. They really couldn't believe their luck when she called back and began to sing for them through the window.

The boys were thrilled. The one on the back of the bike joined in with her. Ariana hooted with laughter.

As they went into a tunnel, cars around them blew their horns at the motorbike to get out of the way, but the duet continued.

"*One last time*," Ariana sang and the light from the boys' smiles could have lit up that dark tunnel.

Ariana had plenty of fans in the media too, with reviewers raving about her powerful voice. Music journalists loved her crystal-clear voice and the way she could skip through octaves. Music had just about taken over her life, but between tour dates Ariana could still dazzle in the TV studio. In 2015, she caused such a stir on *The Tonight Show Starring Jimmy Fallon* that she became a regular guest. Fans of Cat Valentine already knew about Ariana's knack for comedy. Now, viewers all over America were treated to her impish sense of humour and amazing impersonations, on prime-time TV.

In September, Jimmy let her go first to spin the

'Wheel of Musical Impressions' – a game where Jimmy and his guests fight it out for the best impersonations of famous people singing random songs.

"Sooo... it's Britney Spears, who we all know," said Jimmy with a grin. "Singing 'Mary Had a Little Lamb'."

"Mary..." Ariana opened the song, sounding remarkably like Britney Spears from the get-go! Ariana had been impersonating her favourite female singers since she was a little girl, so it was second nature to her and she nailed it effortlessly. The crowd whooped and Jimmy slammed his fist on the table with glee.

Next up for Ariana was impersonating Christina Aguilera singing 'Wheels on the Bus'. Ariana opened up and belted out the famous nursery rhyme as if it were a heartfelt love song. Jimmy leaped out of his chair in amazement. The audience whooped some more.

"We should stop the show there," exclaimed Jimmy when Ariana was done. "That was unbelievable!"

Ariana's performance that night was so good

she was asked to stop by on Jimmy's show again and again. Meanwhile, Ariana did a quick stint on a horror-comedy TV drama called *Scream Queens* – somehow she managed to squeeze the filming into her busy schedule.

Onstage and in television, Ariana had proved that she was top of her game. Yet, something still wasn't right in Ariana's world. She was unhappy about the way women were treated compared to men in the entertainment business. She'd always disagreed with the way female stars were criticised for the clothes they wore or for how they behaved, while male celebrities just got on with things, unchallenged. She also disliked the media's obsession with her love life. Ariana was annoyed that sometimes she was judged more by who she was dating than by her music.

Ariana was a feminist and wanted women to be treated equally – once again, she turned to social media to express her feelings and her tweets caused quite a stir.

"I had to speak out, Nonna," Ariana explained. "I'm lucky enough to be in a position to make a difference. Young girls need to know that they don't need a boyfriend to feel good about themselves. When I said they are *more* than enough on their own, I absolutely meant it."

"I know." Nonna grinned. "And look, you've got millions of female fans – let alone Taylor Swift and Rita Ora – agreeing with you. You go, girl!"

The 'Honeymoon' tour wrapped up in South America in October 2015, but Ariana was no sooner off the stage than she was back on again. Halloween was always one of Ariana's favourite nights of the year – a chance to dress up in masks and make mayhem. That year, Ariana appeared at the iHeartRadio Theater in Los Angeles, singing her latest single 'Focus'. It was an excuse to get into gothic gear and appear in a graveyard dancing with the crew dressed as skeletons!

Afterwards, Ariana went home to host her own Halloween party. This was another excuse for a creepy costume change and to spend time hanging out with friends – her old, for ever friends and the new ones she'd made in the last few years.

"Sometimes I have to pinch myself to make sure it's all real," she confided in Aaron.

"Tonight of all nights, it *isn't* real Ariana," he replied, looking around at everyone dressed up as anything from ghosts to superheroes.

"Ha ha, I love you, Aaron," she laughed. "But you know what I mean. My life is so amazing I can't believe it's real. I'm so lucky and I'm *so* thankful!"

If anyone asked Ariana how she felt about her success at this time, she would tell them how grateful and happy she felt.

"I'm content, because I'm just myself," she told her friend Zach Sang when he interviewed her on his radio show. "It took a while to discover that letting go and just being me is the best way – people can take it or leave it."

"What about your music?" Zack asked.

"I'm a twenty-two-year-old girl, and if I don't write about what I'm feeling then I'm not being genuine. If I didn't write about the things that I'm going through then I'd be sacrificing my artistry," Ariana explained. "It is personal. It has to be."

CHAPTER 21

DANGEROUS WOMAN

Ariana's life was going at a million miles per hour – and that was just in the public eye! Behind the scenes, Ariana was creating her third album. The working title was *Moonlight* and she'd been working on it throughout the year.

Whenever she could, Ariana snatched moments to write her new material – on the tour bus, in between shows, while eating dinner and even in bed. When she did get a few weeks off from touring, she retreated to her home studio to work on her new songs. Inspiration could strike at any time and she'd often record her bright ideas on her phone, so she could work on them later when she finally got time.

When Ariana wasn't performing or recording, she was mixing up even more magic. This time she was making her own fragrance...

"Who knew that music and perfume-making had so much in common?"

Ariana was in the laboratory doing tests for her very own perfume.

"Wow, there are even notes!" she laughed. "In music, when the right notes come together you get a chord; in perfumery you get an *accord* – I love it!"

Ariana's first fragrance was called Ari and it came in a pretty pink bottle with a white fluffy pom-pom. Her followers on Instagram were first to know about it, and when they got their own bottle they were thrilled with its notes of sparkling fruits, florals and marshmallows.

For Christmas 2015, Arianators everywhere had a few must-haves on their wish lists. First was a bottle of Ari perfume and next a copy of her latest holiday EP, *Christmas & Chill*. Ariana had made the EP in just four days, at her home studio in LA. Meanwhile, Ariana spent her Christmas with Joan, Frankie, Nonna and old friends, just cooking and singing, dressing the tree and larking around, like she did in the days before she was famous. Ariana posted to her Snapchat story so her fans could join in with her holiday fun.

However, after a few days off, Ariana was ready to go again.

Giving something back was another important way for Ariana to stay grounded and content. Throughout her career she'd raised money for charity and she was never happier than when she was using her voice to help others. In January 2016, she teamed up with a cosmetics company to launch a lipstick to help raise money for people with AIDS and HIV.

Early that year, Ariana felt happy with how things were going with her new album. Sometimes she felt that making music was like painting a picture. Like an artist, she went back and made changes or touched up something that didn't feel quite right. Ariana was growing up quickly and her style was changing, so she wanted an album title that reflected that. 'Moonlight' was a beautiful song that she was proud of, but it wasn't strong enough as a title for her new album.

"How about *Dangerous Woman*?" Ariana suggested to Frankie.

"What are you trying to say, Ari?" Her brother looked puzzled.

"I want people to pick up the album and know I've changed," she explained. "I want them to see a woman who is not afraid to take a stand. A person happy to be herself and be honest – a dangerous woman!"

'Dangerous Woman', the single, was released in March and was a top ten hit all over the world. Ariana announced on Instagram that she'd reveal one of the songs from the new album's tracklist each day online. When the album was released in May, the fans already knew and loved it well. The musical styles ranged from R&B to reggae and disco to dance. It featured guest stars like Nicki Minaj and Lil Wayne. And, if anyone doubted that Ariana was making a stand, then they only had to look at the front cover. Ariana wore a latex black mask with large bunny ears and a diamond choker around her neck. She claimed to be 'Super Bunny' – someone who could be a superhero or a super villain, depending upon her mood!

Ariana's *Dangerous Woman* was a winner, taking her to number one in the UK album charts for the first time ever. The album hit the top spot all over the world. The fans loved it, and so did many people in the media.

Ariana never allowed criticism of her work to get to her, but even she was pleased when the media were so complimentary.

"I can't believe that those people at the NME have been so sweet," she told Frankie on FaceTime one day. "Listen, they say that my album has 'a message of empowerment that rings true'. That's so awesome – they really get that my feminism is real, Frankie!"

"Hey, listen to this one, Ari." Frankie was reading *andPOP*. "'If there's anything we can take from *Dangerous Woman*, it's that she's growing as an artist. We are obsessed. There's no danger in snatching up this record.'"

"I like this one the most!" Ariana was reading from *Entertainment Weekly*. "'For Grande, giving up on pleasing everybody has only made her more magnetic.'"

Magnetic, magic, moving and amazing – these words were all used to sum up the power of Ariana's performance. Whether it was appearing on the Jimmy Fallon show or *Saturday Night Live* on US television, getting up live at the MTV awards or appearing alongside her childhood hero Madonna at a fundraiser, Ariana could do no wrong. In September, tickets went on sale for the 'Dangerous Woman' tour of 2017 and were quickly sold out.

While tickets flew out of the box offices, Ariana scored another hit. This time, she teamed up with music veteran Stevie Wonder on his single 'Faith'. The song was the lead number for the children's animated film *Sing*, and it was a great get-up-and-go anthem and a brilliant tune to play out another action-packed year.

CHAPTER 22

TOUR, TRAGEDY, TEARS

In the music business, it helps to have faith, but hard work and talent are what get you to the top. On 3 February, 2017, Ariana kicked off her 'Dangerous Woman' tour in Phoenix, Arizona, USA. Each and every concert was epic in its own way. And each song and every dance move was rehearsed many times, to make sure it would be right on the night.

Phoenix was a taste of what was to come on the tour. There was a flood of white stage lights and the dance crew appeared as the opening notes of 'Be Alright' piped up. The dancers were closely followed by Ariana wearing thigh-high boots, a black dress and an immaculate high ponytail. The crowd roared as she burst into beautiful song and effortlessly fell into the dance routine.

Ariana had a talent for picking the right songs, so the set list included old favourites like 'One Last Time', 'Bang Bang', 'Love Me Harder' and 'Problem'. Meanwhile, new material like 'Everyday', 'Let Me Love You', 'Side to Side', 'Into You' and, finally, 'Dangerous Woman' were performed, too. Fabulous costume changes, an on-screen cameo appearance from Nicki Minaj, and the striking visuals on the big screen with the words 'female', 'divine', 'feminist' and 'soulful', gave the show that extra wow factor.

By April, Ariana had toured all over America and Canada, and she had performed the show thirty-seven times. She was more than ready for the next leg of the tour in Europe.

Her gigs in Stockholm, Oslo, Amsterdam, Dublin and Birmingham went down a storm.

On 22 May, Ariana arrived in Manchester, England. She felt excited and relaxed as the parade of young girls in bunny ears streamed into the arena. Everyone backstage had been laughing and joking as always. In the prayer circle before the show, Ariana had wished everyone the best.

"I hope the fans have the best night of their lives," she added.

Ariana had played out the show with the extended version of 'Dangerous Woman'. Then it was time for the goodbyes. As she looked out towards the crowd, she could just about make out the thousands of happy faces of her young fans. Her heart squeezed with tenderness – she always cherished this time at the end of the show. Then hundreds of pink balloons cascaded from the ceiling. The lighting cast a pink-and-magenta glow over the crowd, and everywhere looked so magical – like a dream.

Ariana had just arrived backstage, when she heard a massive bang. For a moment, there was silence. What was that? Ariana's heart began to race. Then the screams started – loud, frightened screams. Ariana wanted to scream, too.

"What was that?" Ariana looked panicked. "What's happening out there?"

Everyone backstage was stunned. Nobody

knew what was going on. But just hearing the piercing screams suggested that something awful had happened.

News about what was happening was broken to Ariana by her mother.

"It's a bomb." Joan's eyes flashed with terror. "I got as many kids backstage with us as possible. I don't know what's going on, but it's frightening out there."

Her mum had been in the front row of the audience that night. Joan had heard the bang and seen smoke. She'd scrambled backstage as quickly as she could, to make sure that Ariana was OK.

What could they do? It was obvious that something horrendous had happened. Ariana felt helpless and collapsed into her mother's arms.

Ariana had lost the power to speak. She opened her mouth, but nothing came out. It was shock. What was happening was unbearable and she needed to tell her fans how sorry she was. Ariana picked up her phone later that night. Typing was easier than speaking, but these were the hardest words ever:

Broken, she wrote on her Twitter feed. As she typed, Ariana held her breath to stop herself from crying. She really didn't have the words to express her sorrow, so that's what she wrote. *From the bottom of my heart, I am so so sorry. I don't have words.*

Ariana was distraught, but she needed to get back home and into the arms of old friends and family. The next day, she landed near Boca Raton. She was devastated and didn't speak for two whole days. The news over the next week only got worse. The explosion at Manchester Arena had caused the death of twenty-two people and injured more than eight hundred others. The stories were heartbreaking, and Ariana felt useless.

Ariana's future was in the balance. She was scared. Could she ever get up and sing again?

Then, one evening, she crawled into her mother's bed and told Joan her big idea.

"I can't imagine never singing again, Mom," she whispered. "I have to sing."

"We Grandes never say never, baby." Joan hugged her close.

"Let's be honest, Mom, I will sing again... but I'm not going to sing again until I sing in Manchester first."

A week later, Ariana returned to Twitter to express her sadness and sorrow for the bereaved families. She sat quietly with her phone, composing a letter that she hoped would show her love and support – although, in truth, she knew there was nothing she could say that would take away the pain that the people of Manchester were feeling.

Somehow, Ariana's words flowed. She wrote about wanting to help: *I extend my hand and heart, and everything I possibly can give, to you and yours.* She also talked about responding to the violence by becoming closer: *to help each other, to love more, to sing louder, to live more kindly and generously than we did before.*

In the same post, Ariana announced that she would return to the *incredibly brave city of Manchester* to meet her fans, visit some of the children in hospital, and host a benefit concert to raise money for the victims and their families. As she put the finishing touches to her message, she knew she had chosen the right path.

Manchester, I promise I won't let you down, she told herself as she tapped the Tweet button.

It was a promise that Ariana took to heart.

Scooter set straight to work, planning the event. Acts like Justin Bieber, Katy Perry and Pharrell Williams were signed up in an instant. Tickets went on sale on 1 June and sold out in six minutes. Ariana landed back in the UK for the One Love: Manchester concert a few days later. She headed straight to the Royal Manchester Children's Hospital to meet some of the young victims.

"Hiii!" Ariana smiled widely as she entered the ward.

The children's faces lit up with surprise.

"Is that really her?" whispered one young girl who had been injured that awful night.

"Hello." Ariana came up to her bed and gave her a sunflower and the softest, cuddliest bear ever.

The child was so shy she could hardly speak, so she giggled instead.

"I'm so proud of you," Ariana told the girl as she gave her a huge hug. "You are so strong and you're doing so well."

The girl's eyes glowed and she giggled again. Meeting Ariana felt like a dream...

CHAPTER 23

SWEETENER

Time is a great healer. These were the very words that Ariana used to make herself feel better as she battled the sadness and anxiety she felt after the Manchester attack.

"Music is supposed to be the safest thing in the world," she told her mum. "I don't think I'll ever find peace with what happened."

"Keep doing what you do best, Ariana," Joan told her. "Use your voice to show that terror cannot win. Remember, love conquers all."

And that was exactly what Ariana did. Two and a half weeks after One Love: Manchester, she resumed the 'Dangerous Woman' tour. Ariana felt nervous when she stepped onto the stage on that first night in Paris. As she looked out towards her audience, she could see thousands of happy faces and hear a chorus of welcoming cheers. She'd nearly been sick in the changing room – it took every bit of her courage and strength of mind to do this, but now she was up here it felt right.

Ariana gulped hard and swallowed the tears that needed to fall. Those tears came later when she sang 'Somewhere Over the Rainbow' and 'One Last Time', which she dedicated to "my twenty-two angels". After the show, she fell into her mother's arms.

"I did it, Mom," she sighed with relief. "I showed them…"

Ariana was just twenty-four years old when she faced such enormous tragedy in her life. Many people were impressed with her dignity and strength. In Paris, the journalist at *Coveteur* asked her about her decision to go ahead with the tour.

"I have never been through anything so traumatic," she replied.

"That is why everyone is so amazed by you," the reporter said. "You are an inspiration to us all. It would have been so much easier to call off the tour."

"Going home was not an option," Ariana told him. "The message of the show was too important. For the crew and everyone involved – it's become more than just a show."

The tour ended in Hong Kong, in September. On that final night, the memory of her "twenty-two angels" moved Ariana to tears again as she sang 'Somewhere Over the Rainbow'. When she left the stage, Ariana experienced a wave of exhaustion. It was like nothing she'd ever felt before – she was physically, emotionally and mentally drained.

For Ariana, life had always been about work, work, work. Now, it was time to go home and rest...

Ariana had become famous for her courage, but inside she was suffering. The stress of what had happened in Manchester had caught up with her and she needed time with her family to heal.

"My anxiety has anxiety," she told Frankie. "I've never felt this bad in my life."

"Time will heal," he reassured her. "That and music!"

"I know – but I don't think I'll ever not think about it and not cry – ever."

When Ariana finally went back to the studio, it felt so right. The past months she'd spent so much time crying and trying to find a way out of the well of despair she felt after Manchester. Now, she was on her real home ground – even the smell of the studio ignited something inside her. She'd spoken with songwriter and producer Savan Kotecha over the phone, and today they just wanted to hang out and play music together. Savan had been involved with her big hits 'Problem' and 'One Last Time', and he made her feel safe, but, most of all, inspired...

"*You* inspire me, Ariana," Savan said. "After everything you've been through, you're back."

"Yep." Ariana smiled. "I'm ready to make the next album, Savan. This is going to be an album of positivity and light. Everyone knows about the tragedy, and I'll go there in my music, but most of all this is an album of hope."

In the background, an old album of Lauryn Hill was playing, and there was something about Lauryn's voice and the great mix of songs that triggered something in both Ariana and Savan.

"I just love her." Ariana had been singing along.

"And the way that the chorus and the verses have different chords. It's complicated, but people don't do that any more – let's do it."

And that was how the extraordinary song 'No Tears Left to Cry' started out. Lauryn was an inspiration and Ariana brought her own light to the music. With its whirl of sounds and chord changes, the song was a breakaway from the average pop song. Listeners could take comfort from Ariana's lyrics, but dance and swirl on the dance floor, too.

Ariana's album was beginning to take shape. Working with Savan and Pharrell Williams had helped Ariana to reconnect with her creativity. But, it wasn't always easy – a song like 'Breathin' sounded like an awesome pop song, but it was inspired by Ariana's panic attacks and was an expression of her deepest anxiety.

'God is a Woman' was Savan's song, but Ariana made it all her own. Joan and Nonna were with her when she recorded it in the studio. That was a truly exciting day: three generations of strong Grande women at the creation of a feminist anthem!

"That is my favourite song of the lot," Nonna

exclaimed when the take was through. "And you know what, I reckon God *is* a woman, too!"

Everyone fell about laughing.

Fans were curious about Ariana – was she OK? Would she ever work again? She'd been out of the public eye for a while. Gradually, Ariana came out of her shell on social media, to reveal a few clues about what she was up to. It was clear that she'd been suffering, but she seemed hopeful, too. Arianators everywhere waited patiently for what she would do next.

At last, in April 2018, the wait was over. Ariana posted a few tear emoticons on social media to herald the release of her new single. 'No Tears Left to Cry' was released a few days later.

"We did it, Savan." Ariana's voice was bursting with excitement. "It's climbing to the top of the charts all over the place!"

"Yeah, Ari." They did a quick fist bump. "You're back!"

"The reviews are just out of this world, too." Ari was reading the review in the British music magazine *NME*. "Listen to this mega one – they say 'Tackling hate and devastation with hope and disco, "No Tears Left to Cry" is a triumph' – it just doesn't get better."

Ariana was turning her life around, but memories of the Manchester attack were always there. That's why she chose to get a tattoo of a bee done – it was tiny, but it said a lot! The worker bee was the symbol of Manchester. She posted a photograph of it to remind everyone that she hadn't forgotten. On the anniversary of the attack, she posted on Twitter to send out love and warmth to the victims. As she did, she broke down again.

"I know I said I've got no more tears to cry – but I do, I really do," she told Joan.

Ariana turned to the camera and swished her platinum blonde ponytail. It was April and she was back on *The Tonight Show with Jimmy Fallon* – and it was terrifying and brilliant all at the same time. If she had to make a comeback, then this was the right place to do it.

Jimmy suggested she come on the show to talk about her new album. Somehow, she'd been persuaded to be a guest for the entire programme. In between the laughter, tears, fan surprises and musical impersonations of Kendrick Lamar, she revealed that the name of her new album was *Sweetener*, and it was due for release in summer 2018.

"Why's it called *Sweetener*?" Jimmy wanted to know.

"Because it's kind of about bringing light to someone's life or someone bringing light to your life – sweetening the situation." Ariana went on to reveal some of the new tracks including 'Raindrop' and Nonna's favourite, 'God is a Woman'.

Fans had to wait until July for the release of 'God is a Woman'. The hip-hop-meets-pop sound hit the right note and was another chart-topper all over the world. Aged twenty-five, Ariana had already achieved so much, but after what had happened in Manchester, what would her album be like – could she live up to her fans' expectations? *Sweetener* was released in August 2018, and fans only had to look at the cover to see that Ariana had changed – the upside-side down photograph of her with platinum blonde hair suggested something new and different.

Ariana had grown up and this album reflected it in many ways. The intro, 'Raindrop (an Angel Cried)', was almost like a hymn, with her beautiful voice soaring and expressing so much pain. From there, she moved on with positive, light-filled pop classics like 'Sweetener' and 'No Tears Left To Cry'. Ariana was also in the mood to experiment and was joined by her childhood musical hero Imogen Heap on 'Goodnight n Go'. Guests like Nicki Minaj and Missy Elliott – and, of course, Pharrell Williams – added to the mix.

The album was loved by the critics as well as fans and reached number one practically everywhere around the world.

"Thanks, Mom," Ariana told Joan as they were curled up on the sofa in her New York apartment. "I wouldn't have got through the past year without you and Nonna."

"And your fans, darling," Joan reminded her.

"Oh yes, they are amazing," Ariana gushed. "I *love* them and I've missed them. I need them as much as they need me. It's like a real love affair, ha ha!"

"A true romance," Joan added.

"I'm so pleased I'm going back on tour again."
Ariana's eyes brightened. "This will be the best
tour ever, Mom!"

In the old days, Ariana fell asleep singing songs
in her head. Sometimes she dreamed about being a
star. These days, she still heard music – but now it
was joined with the cheers from her fans. It was a
beautiful sound, the best ever, and she drifted off
to sleep with a happy, thankful heart.

Turn the page for a sneak preview of another
inspiring Ultimate Superstars story...

BEYONCÉ

CHAPTER 1

SUPER BOWL

Forgetting the words to a song had always been Beyoncé's greatest fear. It had been that way ever since she was a child, performing in talent shows in front of her parents and classmates. Of course, it hardly ever happened – and now, when it did, Bey was pretty good at styling it out.

But the worry still sprung up when she was nervous. And right now, she really was!

Beyoncé quickly pushed the thought away. When she was on tour, she performed to crowds as big as this almost every evening. She was one of the world's most famous entertainers. Standing in front of a crowd of seventy thousand people or more was normal to her!

But today more than 100 million viewers were also watching on TV.

The venue was the Levi's Stadium, Santa Clara, California. The event was Super Bowl 50, the fiftieth anniversary of the iconic American football championship final. The crowd had already watched an action-packed first half of football. The Denver Broncos were beating the Carolina Panthers 13–7. Coldplay had just rocked the stadium with a series of foot-stamping anthems. Now, Bruno Mars and Mark Ronson were onstage, delivering an effortlessly cool performance of their new song, 'Uptown Funk'.

As the song reached its energetic finale, six flares shot up into the sky. The smoke trailed away, then, down on the pitch, a wall of fireworks sizzled into life. This was the drummers' cue to hit their beat.

Boom. Boom. Boom.

Bey waited between the rows of drummers, still hidden from the crowd. She began the countdown in her head, in time with the beat of the drums. *Boom. Boom. Boom. Ten. Nine. Eight.*

The beat got louder and louder. *Seven. Six. Five.*

The drummers began to peel away, to the left and to the right. *Four. Three. Two.*

One. Suddenly Beyoncé was alone, striding up the pitch to the beat of the drums, wearing her trademark bodysuit, her hair billowing behind her like a flame.

Her first notes were soft. Three lines of dancers began to move, one behind Beyoncé, one either side of her, moving together in perfect time. Bey's voice swelled with each line of song. Then, at last, she unleashed its full power. As she did so, columns of yellow flames soared up into the air. The crowd greeted her new song, 'Formation', with wild delight.

Moments later, Bey and her dancers strode off the pitch and onto the stage, facing Bruno Mars and his dancers in a dance-off. The opening notes of 'Crazy in Love' rang through the stadium. This was the song everyone knew – one of Bey's biggest hits.

'Crazy in Love' trailed into 'Uptown Funk' as Beyoncé and Bruno Mars were joined by Coldplay's Chris Martin. Suddenly, the three megastars were singing together. The audience's cheers were at fever pitch.

Then the crowd's attention was directed to the big screen. A video montage showed the most iconic singers who had performed in fifty years of Super Bowl half-time shows: Michael Jackson, Stevie Wonder, Madonna, Bruce Springsteen, Diana Ross, James Brown, Prince and... Beyoncé herself, only four years earlier. Yes, Bey had achieved what just a handful of singers had – she had performed at the Super Bowl twice!

Even for a singer as famous as Bey, it was an amazing feeling to watch herself on the giant screen alongside so many legendary artists. Some of them she had admired since she was a child. These were the greatest singers the world.

And she had earned her place among them.

Life didn't get much bigger or better than this.